Instant Chinese

How to Express Over 1,000 Different Ideas With Just 100 Key Words and Phrases

by Boyé Lafayette De Mente
Revised by Jiageng Fan

WITHDRAWN

D0963746

T**TTLE** Publishing

Tokyo | Rutland, Vermont | Singapore

Contents

PART 2
Additional Vocabulary

Preface

In 1949 the newly established Chinese government issued an edict making Mandarin the national language of the country and mandating that it be taught in all schools. Today, virtually most Chinese speak Mandarin Chinese, known as *putonghua* (puu-toong-whah) or "the common language," as their first or second language.

This book uses English phonetics to represent the syllables making up Mandarin Chinese, making it possible for total newcomers to the language to communicate quickly and easily on a basic level without any previous introduction to the language.

In addition, each Chinese word is given its tone in *pinyin*—this is to enable those with a basic knowledge of Spoken Chinese to say the words more accurately, if they wish. However, for those who know nothing about tones, the phonetic versions presented here are close enough to the "correct" pronunciation that the meaning is generally understandable.

With eight major "dialects" in China [some are actually different enough to be called languages!], the Chinese are used to coping with a variety of accents and variations in the tonal quality of speakers. They are especially tolerant of foreigners who make an effort to speak Chinese, and go out of their way to help them.

Here are a number of important introductory terms to get you started, keeping in mind that the phonetics are designed to be pronounced as English:

China	*Zhōngguó* (*Johng-gwoh*) 中国
Chinese Language	*Hànyǔ* (*Hahn-yuu*) 汉语
	or *Zhōngwén* (*Johng-wern*)* 中文

---

*__Hànyǔ__ is the literary term for the Chinese language; __Zhōngwén__ is the term generally used in ordinary speech.

Chinese (person)	**Zhōngguórén** (*Johng-gwoh-wren*) 中国人
Beijinger	**Běijīngrén** (*Bay-jeeng-wren*) 北京人
Shanghaiese	**Shànghǎirén** (*Shanghai-wren*) 上海人
Overseas Chinese	**Huá Qiáo** (*Hwah Chiaow*) 华侨
Hong Kong	**Xiāng Gǎng** (*She-ahng Gahng*) 香港
Kowloon	**Jiǔlóng** (*Jow-lohng*) 九龙
Macao	**Àomén** (*Ow-mern*) 澳门

PART 1

1   Hello *Nǐ hǎo* *(Nee how)* 你好

Hello! (to one person)
Nǐ hǎo! (Nee how) 你好！

Hello! (to more than one person)
Nǐmen hǎo! (Nee-mern how) 你们好！

Good morning! (until about 10 a.m.)
Nǐ zǎo! (Nee zow) 你早！

Good morning! (very polite form)
Zǎoshang hǎo! (Zow-shahng how) 早上好！

Good afternoon / Good evening!
Nǐ hǎo. (Nee how) 你好！

Good night!
Wǎn ān! (Wahn ahn) 晚安！

Goodbye!
Zài jiàn! (Dzigh jeean) 再见！

2   Thank You *Xièxie* *(Shay-shay)* 谢谢

Thank you.
Xièxie. (Shay-shay) 谢谢。

Thank you very much.
Fēicháng gǎnxiè.
(Fay-chahng gahn-shay) 非常感谢。

Thank you for your hospitality.
Duōxiè nǐ de kuǎndài.
(Dwoh-shay nee der kwahn-die) 多谢你的款待。

No, thanks.
Xièxie, bú yào.
(Shay-shay boo yee-ow) 谢谢，不要。

Don't mention it. / You're welcome.
Búkèqi. (Boo ker-chee) 不客气。

3   Sorry / Excuse Me *bàoqiàn* *(bow-chee-an)* 抱歉

I'm sorry, I apologize.
Duìbuqǐ. (Dway-boo-chee) 对不起。

I'm very sorry.
Wǒ hěn bàoqiàn. (Woh hern bow-chee-an) 我很抱歉。

Excuse me. (to get attention, make way)
Láo jià. (Lao jah) 劳驾。

Excuse me... (May I trouble you)
Máfan nǐ... (Ma-fahn nee...) 麻烦你 …

Excuse me... (May I ask a question)
Qǐng wèn... (Cheeng wern...) 请问 …

4   Please *Qǐng (Cheeng)* 请

Please hurry!
Qǐng gǎnkuài! (Cheeng gahn-kwigh) 请赶快!

Please be careful.
Qǐng xiǎoxīn yìdiǎn.
(Cheeng she-ow-sheen ee-dee-an) 请小心一点。

Come in, please.
Qǐng jìn. *(Cheeng jeen)* 请进。

Please sit down.
Qǐng zuò. *(Cheeng zwoh)* 请坐。

Can you please help me?
Néng bāng wǒ yíxià ma?
(Nerng bahng woh ee-she-ah mah) 能帮我一下吗?

Please write it down.
Qǐng xiě xiàlai. *(Cheeng shay she-ah lie)* 请写下来。

Please write it in Roman letters.
Qǐng yòng pīnyīn xiě.
(Cheeng yohng Peen-een shay) 请用拼音写。

---

5 | I *Wǒ* *(Woh)* 我

I'm an American.
Wǒ shì Měiguórén.
(Woh shr May-gwoh-wren) 我是美国人。

I'm British/English.
Wǒ shì Yīngguórén.
(Woh shr Yeeng-gwoh-wren) 我是英国人。

I am _____.
Wǒ shì _____. *(Woh shr _____)* 我是 _____。

Australian	*Àozhōurén* (Ah-oh-joe-wren) 澳洲人
Canadian	*Jiānádàrén* (Je-ah-nah-dah-wren) 加拿大人
French	*Fǎguórén* (Fa-gwoh-wren) 法国人
German	*Déguórén* (Duh-gwoh-wren) 德国人
Japanese	*Rìběnrén* (Ree-bern-wren) 日本人
Spanish	*Xībānyárén* (She-bahn-yah-wren) 西班牙人

I am from _____.
Wǒ shì _____ lái de. (Woh shr _____ lie-duh)
我是 _____ 来的。

Australia	*Àodàlìyà* (ah-oh-dah-lee-yah) 澳大利亚
Canada	*Jiānádà* (Jah-nah-dah) 加拿大
Denmark	*Dānmài* (Dahn-my) 丹麦
England	*Yīngguó* (Eeng-gwoh) 英国
France	*Fǎguó* (Fah-gwoh) 法国
Germany	*Déguó* (Der-gwoh) 德国
Holland	*Hélán* (Her-lahn) 荷兰
Ireland	*Àiěrlán* (Ay-er-lahn) 爱尔兰
Italy	*Yìdàlì* (Ee-dah-lee) 意大利
Japan	*Rìběn* (Ree-bern) 日本
New Zealand	*Niǔxīlán* (New-she-lahn) 纽西兰
Norway	*Nuówēi* (Noh-way) 挪威
Sweden	*Ruìdiǎn* (Rway-dee-an) 瑞典
Switzerland	*Ruìshì* (Rway-shr) 瑞士
USA	*Měiguó* (May-gwoh) 美国

I'm here on vacation.
Wǒ lái dù jià. (Woh lie doo-jah) 我来渡假。

I'm in China on holiday.
Wǒ lái Zhōngguó lǚxíng.
(Woh lie Johng-gwoh lwee-sheeng) 我来中国旅行。

I'm traveling on business.
Wǒ zuò shēngyi lǚxíng.
(Woh zwoh sherng-ee lwee-sheeng) 我做生意旅行。

I'm in China on business.
Wǒ wèile zuò shēngyi lái Zhōngguó.
(Woh way-ler zwoh sherng-ee lie Johng-gwoh)
我为了做生意来中国。

I am traveling alone.
Wǒ dāndú lǚxíng.
(Woh dahn-doo lwee-sheeng) 我单独旅行。

I don't understand (listening).
Wǒ tīng bù dǒng.
(Woh teeng boo dohng) 我听不懂。

I've had enough, thank you.
Wǒ gòu le, xièxie.
(Woh go ler, shay-shay) 我够了，谢谢。

I know.
Wǒ zhīdào. (Woh jr-dow) 我知道。

I don't know.
Wǒ bù zhīdào. (Woh boo jr-dow) 我不知道。

I'm not sure.
Wǒ bù qīngchu. (Woh boo cheeng-choo) 我不清楚。

I've (already) eaten.
Wǒ chī le. (Woh chr ler) 我吃了。

6 My *Wǒ-de* (Woh-der) 我的

These are my bags.
Zhè shì wǒ-de xíngli.
(Jer shr woh-der sheeng-lee) 这是我的行李。

My address is _____.
Wǒ-de dìzhǐ shì _____.
(Woh-der dee-jr shr_____) 我的地址是 _____。

That is my book.
Zhè shì wǒ-de shū.
(Jer shr woh-der shoo) 这是我的书。

7 You *Nǐ* (Nee)* 你

Are you Chinese?
Nǐ shì Zhōngguórén ma?
(Nee shr Johng-gwoh-wren mah) 你是中国人吗?

Are you Japanese?
Nǐ shì Rìběnrén ma?
(Nee shr Ree-bern-wren mah) 你是日本人吗?

Do you live here?
Nǐ zhù zài zhè ge dìfang ma? 你住在这个地方吗?
(Nee joo dzigh jay-guh dee-fahng mah)

Are you married?
Nǐ jiéhūn le ma?
(Nee jay-hoon-ler mah) 你结婚了吗?

Do you have children?
Nǐ yǒu háizi le ma?
(Nee you high-dzu-ler mah) 你有孩子了吗?

*The "you" (*nǐ*) is generally left out of sentences when it is understood from the context.

8   Yes / No* *Shì* (shr) 是 / *Bù* (Boo) 不

*"Yes" and "No" are not commonly used on their own in Chinese. "Yes" is usually expressed by repeating the verb. The negative is expressed by putting *bù (boo)* or *méi (may)* in front of verbs and adjectives.

9   Names *Míngzi* (Meeng-dzu) 名字

first name	*míng (meeng)* 名
family name	*xìng (sheeng)* 姓

What is your first name?
Nǐ guì míng? (Neen gway-meeng) 你贵名?

What is your family name?
Nǐ xìng shénme? (Nee sheeng shern-mo) 你姓什么?

My family name is _____.
Wǒ xìng _____. (Woh sheeng _____) 我姓 _____。

10 We Wǒmen *(Woh-mern)* 我们

Where are we? / Where is this?
Zhè shì nǎli? (Jer shr nah-lee?) 这是哪里?

We are not going.
Wǒmen bú qù. (Woh-mern boo chwee) 我们不去。

We have one daughter.
Wǒmen yǒu yígè nǚér.
(Woh-mern you ee-guh nwee-urr) 我们有一个女儿。

We live in America.
Wǒmen zhù Měiguó.
(Woh-mern joo May-gwoh) 我们住美国。

We are married.
Wǒmen jiéhūn le.
(Woh-mern jeh-hoon-ler) 我们结婚了。

We want to go to _____.
Wǒmen yào qù _____.
(Woh-mern yee-ow chwee _____) 我们要去 _____。

11 Speak Shuō *(Shwo)*

Do you speak English?
Nǐ huì shuō Yīngwén ma?
(Nee hway shwo Eeng-wern mah?) 你会说英文吗?

I don't speak Chinese.
Wǒ búhuì Zhōngwén.
(Woh boo hway Johng-wern) 我不会中文。

I speak a little Chinese.
Huì yīdiǎn Zhōngwén.
(Hway ee-dee-an Johng-wern) 会一点中文。

Please speak more slowly.
Qǐng shuō màn yīdiǎn.
(Cheeng shwo mahn ee-dee-an) 请说慢一点。

What did you say?
Nǐ shuō shénme?
(Nee shwo shern-mo) 你说什么?

Please repeat that.
Qǐng nǐ zàishuō yībiàn.
(Cheeng nee dzie shwo ee-bee-an?) 请你再说一遍。

What did he say?
Tā shuō shénme?
(Tah shwo shern-mo) 他说什么?

12 Understand *Dǒng* *(Dohng)* 懂

I understand.
Wǒ dǒng. *(Woh dohng)* 我懂。

I don't understand.
Wǒ bù dǒng. *(Woh boo dohng)* 我不懂。

We don't understand.
Wǒmen bù dǒng. *(Woh-mern boo dohng)* 我们不懂。

Do you understand?
Nǐ dǒng ma? *(Nee dohng mah)* 你懂吗?

Did you understand?
Nǐ míngbai le ma?
(Nee meeng by-ler mah) 你明白了吗?

I need an interpreter.
Wǒ xūyào fānyì.
(Woh she-yow fahn-ee ywahn) 我需要翻译。

---

13 **Who?** (question) *Shuí* *(Shway)* 谁?

Who are you?
Nǐ shì shuí? (Nee shr shway) 你是谁?

Who is that?
Nà shì shuí? (Nah shr shway) 那是谁?

Who is first?
Shuí shì dìyī ge?
(Shway shr-dee ee-guh) 谁是第一个?

Who speaks English?
Shuí néng shuō Yīngwén?
(Shway nerng shwo Eeng-wern) 谁能说英文?

---

14 **What?** *Shénme?* *(Shern-mo)* 什么?

What is this called in Chinese?
Zhège Zhōngwén jiào shénme?
(Jay-guh Johng-wern jow shern-mo) 这个中文叫什么?

What is that called?
Nàge jiào shénme?
(Nah guh jee-ow shern-mo) 那个叫什么?

What time is breakfast?
Jǐdiǎn chī zǎofàn?
(Jee-dee-an chr zow-fahn) 几点吃早饭?

What time is lunch?
Jǐdiǎn chī wǔfàn? (Jee-dee-an chr woo-fahn)
几点吃午饭?

What is your address?
Nǐ de dìzhǐ? (Nee-der dee-jr) 你的地址?

What is this street?
Zhè shì něi tiáo jiē?
(Jur shr nay-tee-ow jeh) 这是哪条街?

What is that?
Nà shì shénme?
(Nah shr shern-mo) 那是什么?

When? *Shénme shíhou?* *(Shern-mo shr-hoe)*
什么时候?

When are we going?
Wǒmen shénme shíhou qù?
(Woh-mern shern-mo shr-hoe chwee) 我们什么时候去?

When will you be finished?
Nǐ shénme shíhou huì hǎo?
(Nee shern-mo shr-hoe hway how) 你什么时候会好?

When does it begin?
Shénme shíhou kāishǐ ?
(Shern-mo shr-hoe kigh-shr?) 什么时候开始?

Where? *Nǎlǐ?* (Nah-lee) 哪里?/ *Nǎr?*
(Nah-urr) 哪儿?

Where is ____?
____ *zài nǎ?* (____ *zigh nah-urr*) ____ 在哪?

Where is it?
Tā zài nǎlǐ? (Tah zigh nah-lee) 它在哪里?

Where do you live?
Nǐ zhù zài nǎ? (Nee joo zigh nah?) 你住在哪?

Where are you from?
Nǐ shì cóng nǎ lái de?
(Nee shr tsohng nah-urr lie-der) 你是从哪来的?

Where do you want to go?
Nǐ xiǎng qù nǎlǐ?
(Nee she-ahng chwee nah-lee) 你想去哪里?

Where are we going?
Wǒmen yào qù nǎlǐ?
(Woh-mern yow chwee nah-lee) 我们要去哪里?

Where is my friend?
Wǒ-de péngyou zài nǎlǐ?
(Woh-der perng-you zigh nah-lee) 我的朋友在哪里?

Where is the bus stop?
Chēzhàn zài nǎlǐ?
(Cher jahn zigh nah-lee) 车站在哪里?

17 **Why?** *Wèishénme?* (Way shern-mo) 为什么?

Why? (whenever needed)
Wèishénme? (Way-shern-mo) 为什么?

18 **How?** *Duō?* (Dwoh) 多; *Zěnme?* (Zern-mo) 怎么?

How much is it / that?
Duōshao qián? (Dwoh shou chee-an) 多少钱?

How much is this?
Zhè shì duōshao? (Jur shr dwoh-shou) 这是多少?

How does this work?
Zhè zěnme cāozuò? (Jur zern-mo chow zwoh)
这怎么操作?

How far is it?
Lí zhè duō yuǎn? (Lee juh dwoh ywahn)
离这多远?

How long will it take?
Zhè yào duō jiǔ? (Juh yow dwoh jeo) 这要多久?

19 **This** *Zhè* (Jur) 这; *Zhèi* (Jay) 这

This is mine.
Zhè shì wǒde. (Jur shr woh-der) 这是我的。

What is this?
Zhè shì shénme? (Juh shr shern-mo) 这是什么?

I don't like this (it).
Bù xǐhuan. (Boo she-hwahn) 不喜欢。

How much is this?
Zhè shì duōshao? (Jur shr dwoh-shou) 这是多少?

This is very good.
Zhè hěn hǎo. (Jur hern how) 这很好。

20 | That Nà (Nah) 那/ Nèi (Nay) 哪

What is that?
Nà shì shénme?
(Nah shr shern-mo) 那是什么?

That's my luggage.
Nà shì wǒde xíngli.
(Nah shr woh-der sheeng-lee) 那是我的行李。

Is that so?
Shì ma? (Shr mah) 是吗?

How much is that?
Nà shì duōshao?
(Nah shr dwoh-shou) 那是多少?

Who is / was that?
Nà shì shéi? (Nah shr shay) 那是谁?

What is that street?
Nà shì něi tiáo jiē?
(Nah shr nay-tee-ow jeh) 那是哪条街?

21 Write *Xiě* (Shay) 写

Please write it down.
Qǐng nǐ xiě xià. (Cheeng nee shay shah) 请你写下。

Please write it in Roman letters.
Qǐng yòng pīnyīn xiě.
(Cheeng yohng peen-yeen shay) 请用拼音写。

Please write it in Chinese.
Qǐng yòng Zhōngwén xiě.
(Cheeng yohng Johng-wern shay) 请用中文写。

22 Address *Dìzhǐ* (dee-jr) 地址

(This is) my address.
Wǒ-de dìzhǐ. (Woh-der dee-jr) 我的地址。

What is your address?
Nǐ-de zhùzhǐ shì?
(Nee-der joo jr shr) 你的住址是?

Please give me your address.
Qǐng gàosu wǒ nǐ de dìzhǐ. 请告诉我你的地址。
(Cheeng gow-soo woh nee der dee-jr)

My home address is ...
Wǒ jiā de dìzhǐ shì...
(Woh-jee-ah der dee-jr shr...) 我家的地址是 …

Please write it down.
Qǐng xiě xià lai. (Cheeng shay shah lie) 请写下来。

Please read it to me.
Qǐng dú zhè ge gěi wǒ tīng.
(Cheeng doo jur-guh guy-woh ting) 请读这个给我听。

Please read it out loud.
Qǐng dàshēng dú.
(Cheeng dah sherng doo) 请大声读。

23 Introductions *Jièshào* *(Jeh-shou)* 介绍

May I introduce myself?
Wǒ kěyǐ jièshào wǒ zìjǐ ma? 我可以介绍我自己吗?
(Woh ker-ee jeh-shou woh-dzu-jee mah)

My name is _____.
Wǒ de míngzi shì _____.
(Woh-der meeng-dzu shr _____) 我的名字是 _____。

This is my name card.
Zhè shì wǒ de míngpiàn.
(Jur shr woh-der meeng pee-an) 这是我的名片。

What is your name?
Nǐ jiào shénme míngzi?
(Nee jow shern-mo meeng-dzu) 你叫什么名字?

I'm pleased to meet you.
Jiǔ yǎng. (Joe-yahng) 久仰。

Do you have a name card?
Nǐ yǒu míngpiàn ma?
(Nee you meeng pee-an mah) 你有名片吗?

This is my wife.
Zhè shì wǒ de fūren.
(Jur shr woh-der foo-wren) 这是我的夫人。

24   **Family** *Jiārén (jah-wren)* 家人

husband	*zhàngfu (jahng-foo)* 丈夫
wife	*fūren (foo-wren)* 夫人
	qīzi (chee-dzu) 妻子
children	*háizi (high-dzu)* 孩子
daughter	*nǚér (nwee-urr)* 女儿
son	*érzi (urr-dzu)* 儿子

Do you have children?
Yǒu háizi ma? (You high-dzu mah) 有孩子吗?

I have two daughters.
Yǒu liǎngge nǚér.
(You lee-ahng-guh nwee-urr) 有两个女儿。

Are you married?
Jiéhūn le ma?
(Jeh hoon-ler mah) 结婚了吗?

I'm married.
Jiéhūn le. (Jeh hoon-ler) 结婚了。

I'm single.
Méi jiéhūn. (May jeh-hoon) 没结婚。

This is my wife.
Zhè wèi shì wǒ qīzi.
(Jur-way shr woh chee-dzu) 这位是我妻子。

This is my husband.
Zhè wèi shì wǒ zhàngfu.
(Jur-way shr woh jahng-foo) 这位是我丈夫。

25 Age *Niánlíng* *(Nee-an-leeng)* 年龄; *Suì* *(Sway)* 岁

How old are you? (to young children)
Nǐ jǐ suì? *(Nee jee sway)* 你几岁?

How old are you? (to all others)
Nǐ duōdà? *(Nee dwoh dah)* 你多大?

26 Go *Qù* *(Chwee)* 去

I am going.
Qù. *(Chwee)* 去。

I'm not going.
Bú qù. *(Boo chwee)* 不去。

Are you going?
Nǐ qù ma? *(Nee chwee mah)* 你去吗?

Is he/she going
Tā qù ma? *(Tah chwee mah)* 他／她去吗?

Are they going?
Tāmen qù ma? *(Tah-mern chwee mah)* 他们去吗?

Are we going now?
Wǒmen xiànzài qù ma?
(Woh-mern shee-an-zigh chwee mah) 我们现在去吗?

27 Come *Lái* *(Lie)* 来

I'm coming.
Wǒ lái. (Woh lie) 我来。

I'm not coming.
Wǒ bù lái. (Woh boo lie) 我不来。

He/she is coming.
Tā lái. (Tah lie) 他／她来。

He/she is not coming.
Tā bù lái. (Tah boo lie) 他／她不来。

I cannot come.
Bùnéng lái. (Boo nerng lie) 不能来。

They are coming.
Tāmen lái. (Tah-mern lie) 他们来。

I will come tomorrow.
Wǒ míngtiān lái. (Woh meeng-tee-an lie) 我明天来。

Please come to my home/house.
Qǐng lái wǒ jiā zuò zuò.
(Cheeng lie woh-jee-ah zwoh-zwoh) 请来我家坐坐。

28 Toilet *Cèsuǒ* *(Tser-swoh)* 厕所

men	*nán (nahn)* 男	
women	*nǚ (nwee)* 女	
public toilet	*gōnggòng cèsuǒ*	
	(gohng-gohng tser-swoh) 公共厕所	

Where is the toilet, please?
Qǐngwèn, cèsuǒ zǎi nǎr? 请问，厕所在哪儿?
(Cheeng-wern, tser-swoh dzigh nah-urr)

Is there a public toilet near here?
Zhè fùjìn yǒu gōnggòng cèsuǒ ma?
(Jur foo-jeen you gohng-gohng tser-swoh mah)
这附近有公共厕所吗?

I need to go to the toilet.
Wǒ yào qù cèsuǒ.
(Woh yee-ow chwee tser-swoh) 我要去厕所。

29	**Money** *Qián* (Chee-an) 钱	

Chinese currency	*Rénmínbì* (wren-meen-bee) 人民币	
US dollars	*Měiyuán* (May ywahn) 美元	
Hong Kong dollars	*Gǎngbì* (Gahng bee) 港币	
Australian dollars	*Àodàlìyàyuán* 澳大利亚元 (Ah-aw-dah-lee-yah ywen)	
Canadian dollars	*Jiābì* (Jee-ah-bee) 加币	
English pounds	*Yīngbàng* (Yeeng bahng) 英镑	
Japanese yen	*Rìyuán* (Ree ywahn) 日元	
travelers' checks	*lǚxíng zhīpiào* 旅行支票 (lwee-sheeng jr-pee-ow)	
credit cards	*xìnyòngkǎ* (sheen-yohng kah) 信用卡	
cash	*xiànkuǎn* (shee-an-kwahn) 现款	

Where can I exchange money?
Nǎlǐ kěyǐ duìhuàn qián? 哪里可以兑换钱?
(Nah-lee ker-ee dway-hwahn chee-an)

What is today's exchange rate for US dollars?
Jīntiān měiyuán duìhuàn lǜ duōshao?
(Jeen-tee-an May ywahn dway-hwahn lwee dwoh-shou) 今天美元兑换率多少?

Can you write it down?
Nǐ néng xiě xiàlai ma?
(Nee nung shay-she-ah lie mah) 你能写下来吗?

Credit Cards *Xìnyòngkǎ* (Sheen-yohng kah)
信用卡

Do you accept credit cards?
Nǐ shōu xìnyòngkǎ ma?
(Nee show sheen-yohng kah mah) 你收信用卡吗?

Which credit cards do you accept?
Nǐmen jiēshòu nǎxiē xìnyòngkǎ?
(Nee-mern jeh-show nah-shay sheen-yohng kah)
你们接受哪些信用卡?

Can I use my credit card to get cash?
Wǒ néng yòng xìnyòngkǎ qǔ xiànjīn ma?
(Woh nerng yohng sheen-yohng kah chwee shee-an ma) 我能用信用卡取现金吗?

Want *Yào* *(Yow)* 要

I want to go to the Great Wall.
Wǒ yào qù Chángchéng.
(Woh yow chwee Chahng Cherng) 我要去长城。

I want to go sightseeing.
Wǒ yào qù guānguāng.
(Woh yow chwee gwahn-gwahng) 我要去观光。

I want to buy a newspaper.
Wǒ yào mǎi bàozhǐ.
(Woh yow my bow-jr) 我要买报纸。

I want to go to the American Embassy.
Wǒ yào qù Měiguó dàshǐguǎn. 我要去美国大使馆。
(Woh yow chwee May-gwoh Dah-shr-gwahn)

I want to rest.
Wǒ yào xiūxi.
(Woh yee-ow she-oh-she) 我要休息。

Need *Xūyào* *(She-yee-ow)* 需要

I need some aspirin.
Wǒ xūyào āsīpǐlín.
(Woh she-yee-ow ahs-pee-leen) 我需要阿司匹林。

I need some foot powder.
Wǒ xūyào jiǎozhǐ fěn.
(Woh she-yee-ow jee-ow chee fern) 我需要脚趾粉。

I need some shampoo.
Wǒ xūyào xǐfàjì.
(Woh she-yee-ow see-fa-jee) 我需要洗发剂。

I need some razor blades.
Wǒ xūyào guāhú dāo.
(Woh she-yee-ow gwah-hoo dow) 我需要刮胡刀。

I need some eyedrops.
Wǒ xūyào yǎn yàoshuǐ.
(Woh she-yee-ow yahn-yee-ow shway) 我需要眼药水。

I need an umbrella.
Wǒ xūyào yǔsǎn.
(Woh she-yee-ow yuh-sahn) 我需要雨伞。

33 Airport *Fēijīchǎng* *(Fay-jee-chahng)* 飞机场

airport shuttle bus	*jīchǎng jiē sòng chē* *(jee-chahng jee-eh sohng-cher)* 机场接送车
airplane	*fēijī* *(fay-jee)* 飞机
airline	*hángkōnggōngsī* 航空公司 *(hahng-kohng-gohng-suh)*
hotel shuttle bus	*lǚguǎn jiē sòng chē* 旅馆接送车 *(lwee-gwahn jee-eh sohng-cher)*
flight number	*hángbān hàomǎ* 航班号码 *(hahng-bahn how-mah)*
reservations	*yùdìng* *(yuu-deeng)* 预定
ticket	*piào* *(pee-ow)* 票
first-class	*tóuděng cāng* *(toe-derng tsahng)* 头等舱

first-class ticket	*tóuděng piào*
	(toe-derng pee-ow) 头等票
economy class	*jīngjì cāng*
	(jeeng-jee tsahng) 经济舱
economy class ticket	*pǔtōng piào*
	(poo-tohng pee-ow) 普通票
confirm	*quèrèn (chwee-uh-wren)* 确认
connecting flight	*xiánjiē hángbān* 衔接航班
	(shee-an jee-eh hahng-bahn)
boarding card	*dēngjī kǎ*
	(derng-jee kah) 登机卡
carry-on baggage	*shǒutíbāo*
	(show-tee bow) 手提包
aisle seat	*kào zǒudào zuòwèi*
	(kow-zow dow zwoh-way)
	靠走道坐位
window seat	*kào chuāng zuòwèi* 靠窗座位
	(kow-chwahng zwoh-way)
passport	*hùzhào (hoo-jow)* 护照

Please help me with my luggage.
Qǐng nǐ bāng wǒ bān xíngli. 请你帮我搬行李。
(Cheeng nee bahng woh bahn sheeng-lee)

Where do I wait for the hotel shuttle bus?
Zài nǎli děng lǚguǎn de bāshì?
(Dzigh nah-lee derng lwee-gwahn der ba-shr)
在哪里等旅馆的巴士?

Is this the queue for the shuttle bus?
Zài zhèlǐ páiduì děng lǚguǎn bāshì ma?
(Dzigh jur-lee pah-dway derng-gwahn ba-shr mah)
在这里排队等旅馆巴士吗?

Where can I get a taxi?
Nǎlǐ yǒu chūzū chē?
(Nah-lee you choo-joo cher) 哪里有出租车?

From 2014, the Chinese government have begun to loosen the visa requirement of international travelers. If you are transiting, chances are that you no longer need a transit visa in major airports. For group travelers, you may not need to apply for a visa at all (especially for Hainan province).

At the Customs   *hǎiguān* (high-gwahn) 海关

Here is my passport.
Zhè shì wǒde hùzhào.
(Juh shr woh-der hoo-jow) 这是我的护照。

Here is my arrival card.
Zhè shì wǒde rùjìngkǎ.
(Jur shr woh-der roo-jeeng-kah) 这是我的入境卡。

Here is my departure card.
Zhè shì wǒde chūjìngkǎ.
(Jur shr woh-der choo-jeeng-kah) 这是我的出境卡。

My purpose (of visit) is business.
Wǒ lái Zhōngguó shāngwù lǚxíng.
(Woh lie johng-gwoh shahng-woo lu-sheeng)
我来中国商务旅行。

My purpose (of visit) is sightseeing.
Wǒ lái guānguāng.
(Woh lie gwahn-gwahng) 我来观光。

I have items (don't have any item) to declare.
Wǒ yǒu / méiyǒu wùpǐn shēnbào. (Woh you / may-you woo-peen shern-bow) 我有／没有物品申报。

I intend to stay in China for ... days.
Wǒ yùjì huì zài Zhōngguó ... tiān.
(Woh yuu-jee hway zigh johng-gwoh... tee-an)
我预计会在中国…天。

34 Tip *Xiǎofèi* (Shou-fay) 小费

Is tipping permitted here?
Zhèlǐ kěyǐ gěi xiǎofèi ma?
(Jur-lee ker-ee gay shou-fay mah? 这里可以给小费吗?

How much should I tip?
Yīnggāi gěi duōshao xiǎofèi?
(Yeeng-guy gay dwoh-shou shou-fay) 应该给多少小费?

This tip is for you.
Zhè xiǎofèi shì gěi nǐ de.
(Jur shou-fay shr gay nee-der) 这小费是给你的。

35 Taxi *Chūzūchē* (Choo-joo-cher) 出租车

taxi stand	*chūzūchē zhàn* *(choo joo cher jahn)* 出租车站
fare	*piào jià (pee-ow-jah)* 票价

Where can I get a taxi?
Chūzūchē zài nǎr?
(Choo-joo cher dzigh nah-urr) 出租车在哪儿?

Is there a taxi stand near here?
Zhè fùjìn yǒu chūzūchē zhàn ma?
(Jur foo-jeen yow choo-joo cher jahn mah)
这附近有出租车站吗?

Please call a taxi for me.
Qǐng gěi wǒ jiào chē.
(Cheen gay woh jow cher) 请给我叫车。

I want to go to _____.
Wǒ yào qù _____.
(Woh yow chwee _____) 我要去_____。

Please take me to _____.
Qǐng sòng wǒ dào _____.
(Cheeng sohng woh dow _____) 请送我到_____。

Please take me to the airport.
Qǐng dài wǒ dào fēijīchǎng. 请带我到飞机场。
(Cheeng die woh dow fay-jee chahng)

The airport, please.
Qǐng qù jīchǎng.
(Cheeng chwee jee-chahng) 请去机场。

I'm in a hurry.
Wǒ gǎn shíjiān.
(Woh gahn shr-jee-ann) 我赶时间。

How long will it take to get to the airport?
Dào jīchǎng yào duōshao shíjiān?
(Dow jee-chahng yow dwoh-shou shr-jee-an?)
到机场要多少时间?

Please take me to my hotel.
Qǐng dài wǒ dào wǒde lǚguǎn. 请带我到我的旅馆。
(Cheeng die woh dow woh-der lwee-gwahn)

Please pick me up at _____.
Qǐng dào _____jiē wǒ.
(Cheeng dow _____ jee-eh woh) 请到 _____ 接我。

Please come back at ____.
Qǐng ____ huílai.
(Cheeng ____ hwee lie) 请 ____ 回来。

Please take me to this address.
Qǐng dài wǒ dào zhège dìzhǐ. 请带我到这个地址。
(Cheeng die woh dow jay-guh dee-jr)

Please go to Tiananmen Square.
Qǐng qù Tiānānmén Guǎngchǎng. 请去天安门广场。
(Cheeng chwee Tee-an-ahn-mern Gwahng Chahng)

Can you wait for me?
Nǐ néng děng wǒ ma?
(Nee nerng derng woh mah) 你能等我吗?

Please wait for me.
Qǐng nǐ děng yī děng.
(Cheeng nee derng ee derng) 请你等一等。

How much do I owe you?
Gāi fù duōshao qián?
(Guy foo dwoh-shou chee-an) 该付多少钱?

How much?
Duōshao qián? (Dwoh shou chee-an) 多少钱?

Bus *Qìchē* (Chee-cher) 汽车

central bus station	*qìchē zǒng zhàn* (chee-cher zohng jahn) 汽车总站
bus station	*gōnggòng chēzhàn* 公共车站 (gohng-gohng-chee-cher jahn)
bus stop	*qìchē zhàn* (cher jahn) 汽车站

Is there a bus stop near here?
Zhè fùjìn yǒu qìchē zhàn ma? 这附近有汽车站吗?
(Jr foo-jeen yow chee-cher jahn mah)

Where is the bus station?
Gōnggòngqìchē zhàn zài nǎlǐ? 公共汽车站在哪里?
(Gohng-gohng chee-cher jahn dzigh nah-lee)

How do I get to the bus station?
Dào qìchē zhàn zěnme zǒu? 到汽车站怎么走?
(Dow chee-cher jahn zern-mah dzow)

Which bus do I take to get to Tiananmen Square?
Dào Tiānānmén zuò jǐ lù chē? 到天安门坐几路车?
(Dow Tee-an-ahn-mern zwoh jee loo cher)

Is it necessary to change buses?
Yào huàn chē ma? (Yow hwahn cher mah) 要换车吗?

How much is the fare?
Piào jià duōshao?
(Pee-ow jah dwoh-shou) 票价多少?

Do you have a map/brochure of the city?

Nǐmen yǒu méiyǒu běn shì dìtú / jièshào shū?

(Nee-mern you may-you bern shr dee-too /jee-eh-shaow shoo) 你们有没有本市地图／介绍书?

Please give me a bus timetable.

Qǐng gěi wǒ yīgè gōnggòng qìchē shíkèbiǎo.

(Cheeng gay woh ee-guh gohng-gohng chee-cher shr-ker beow) 请给我一个公共汽车时刻表。

Please take me to the bus station.

Qǐng dài wǒ dào gōnggòng qìchē zhàn.

(Cheeng die woh dow gohng-gohng chee cher-jahn) 请带我到公共汽车站。

Where does the bus for downtown / the airport leave from?

Qù chéng lǐ / fēijīchǎng de gōnggòng qìchē cóng nǎr kāi?

(Chwee cherng-lee / fay-jee-chahng der gohng-gohng chee-cher tsohng narr kigh) 去 城里／飞机场 的公共汽车从哪儿开?

Is this the bus for the airport?

Zhè shì bùshì qù jīchǎng de gōnggòng qìchē?

(Jay shr boo shr chwee jee-chahng der gohng-gohng chee-cher) 这是不是去机场的公共汽车?

How much is it to the airport?

Qù fēijīchǎng duōshao qián? 去飞机场多少钱?

(Chwee fay-jee-chahng dwoh-shou chee-an)

What time is the bus leaving?

Gōnggòng qìchē jǐdiǎn kāi? 公共汽车几点开?

(Gohng-gohng chee-cher jee-dee-an kigh)

37 Subway *Dìtiě* (Dee-tee-eh) 地铁

subway station	*dìtiě zhàn* (dee-tee-eh jahn) 地铁站
subway ticket	*dìtiě piào* (dee-tee-eh pee-ow) 地铁票
subway card*	*dìtiěkǎ* (dee-tee-eh kah) 地铁卡

*for multiple travels' commuters

subway ticket machine	*dìtiě shòupiàojī* 地铁售票机 (dee-tee-eh show-pee-ow jee)
light rail transit/ LRT	*qīngguǐ* (cheeng-gway) 轻轨
LRT station	*qīngguǐ zhàn* (cheeng-gway jahn) 轻轨站

Where is the nearest subway station?
Zuìjìn de dìxià tiěchē zhàn zài nǎlǐ?
(Zway-jeen der dee-shah-tee-eh cher jahn zigh nah-lee) 最近的地下铁车站在哪里?

Let's go by subway.
Wǒmen zuò dìxià tiě qù. 我们坐地下铁去。
(Woh-mern zwoh dee-shah-tee-eh chwee)

How much is the subway ticket?
Dìtiě piào duōshao qián? 地铁票多少钱?
(Dee-tee-eh pee-ow dwoh-shou chee-in)

I'd like a monthly pass.
Wǒ xiǎng mǎi yuè piào.
(Woh shee-ahng my yu-eh pee-ow) 我想买月票。

I'd like one adult ticket.
Wǒ xiǎng mǎi yīzhāng chéngrén piào.
(Woh shee-ahng my ee-jahng churng-wren pee-ow)
我想买一张成人票。

I'd like one child/senior ticket.
Wǒ xiǎng mǎi yīzhāng értóng / lǎonián piào.
(woh shee-ahng my ee-jahng ern-tohng/lao-nee-an pee-ow) 我想买一张儿童／老年票。

When is the last train?
Zuìhòu yībānchē jǐdiǎn? 最后一班车几点？
(Zway-hoe ee-bahn cher jee-dee-an)

38 Train *Huǒchē* (Hwoh-cher) 火车

China National Railways	*Zhōngguó tiělù* 中国铁路 *(Johng-gwoh Tee-eh-loo)*
Maglev (magnetic levitation)	*cí xuánfú* *(tsu shwen-foo)* 磁悬浮
HST (High-speed Train)	*gāotiě* *(gow-tee-eh)* 高铁
bullet-train	*dòngchē* *(doong-cher)* 动车
train station	*huǒchē zhàn* *(hwoh-cher jahn)* 火车站
local (ordinary) train	*pǔtōng chē* *(poo-tohng cher)* 普通车
express train	*kuàichē* *(kwie cher)* 快车
slow train	*màn chē* *(mahn cher)* 慢车
train ticket	*chē piào* *(cher-pee-ow)* 车票
ticket office	*shòupiào chù* *(show pee-ow choo)* 售票处

one-way ticket	*dānchéng piào*
	(dahn cherng pee-ow) 单程票
round-trip ticket	*láihuí piào*
	(lie-hway pee-ow) 来回票
first-class ticket	*tóuděng piào*
	(toe-derng pee-ow) 头等票
economy-class ticket	*pǔtōng piào*
	(poo-tohng pee-ow) 普通票
soft-class (ticket)	*ruǎnzuò (rwahn zwoh)* 软座
hard-class (ticket)	*yìngzuò (eeng zwoh)* 硬座
soft sleeper	*ruǎnwò pù*
	(rwahn woh poo) 软卧铺
hard sleeper	*yìngwò pù*
	(eeng woh poo) 硬卧铺
compartment	*chēxiāng (cher-she-ahng)* 车厢
reserved seat ticket	*yùdìng zuòwèi piào* 预定座位票
	(yuu-deeng zwoh-way pee-ow)
unreserved seat ticket	*wú yùdìng zuòwèi piào*
	(woo yuu-deeng zwoh-way pee-ow) 无预定座位票
fare	*chēfèi (cher-fay)* 车费
boarding platform	*yuètái (yuu-eh-tie)* 月台
dining car	*cān chē (tsan cher)* 餐车
transfer	*dǎo / huàn*
	(dow / hwahn) 倒 / 换
get on (board)	*shàng chē (shahng cher)* 上车
get off (disembark)	*xià chē (she-ah cher)* 下车

Where is the train station?
Chēzhàn zài nǎlǐ?
(Cher jahn zigh nah-lee) 车站在哪里?

Where is the ticket office?
Nǎlǐ shì shòupiào chù?
(Nah-lee shr show pee-ow choo) 哪里是售票处?

I want to go to _____.
Wǒ yào qù _____ .
(Woh yow chwee _____) 我要去_____。

What is the track number?
Jǐ hào huǒchē?
(Jee how hwoh-cher) 几号火车?

What is the track number for the train going to Beijing?
Qù Běijīng de huǒchē zài jǐ hào tái?
(Chwee Beijing der hwoh-cher zigh jee how tie)
去北京的火车在几号台?

How do I get to the train station?
Dào huǒchē zhàn zěnme zǒu?
(Dow hwoh-cher jahn zern-mo dzow)
到火车站怎么走?

Please take me to the train station.
Qǐng dài wǒ dào huǒchē zhàn. 请带我到火车站。
(Cheeng die woh dow hwoh-cher jahn)

Do you have a railway timetable, please.
Qǐng gěi wǒ yīgè huǒchē shíkèbiǎo.
(Cheeng gay woh ee-guh hwoh-cher shr-ker-beow)
请给我一个火车时刻表。

When does the train leave for Shanghai?
Qù Shànghǎi de huǒchē jǐdiǎn kāi?
(Chwee Shang-hai der hwoh-cher jee-dee-an kigh)
去上海的火车几点开?

Where do I buy a ticket?
Piào zài nǎr mǎi?
(Pee-ow dzigh nah-urr my) 票在哪儿买?

Do I have to transfer anywhere?
Wǒ jiāng zài nǎlǐ huàn chē? 我将在哪里换车?
(Woh jee-ahng zigh nah-lee hwan-cher)

Walk / Stroll *Zǒu* (Dzow) 走 / *Sànbù* (Sahn-boo) 散步

39

Let's go for a stroll.
Wǒmen qù sànbù.
(Woh-mern chwee sahn-boo) 我们去散步。

I prefer to walk.
Wǒ xǐhuan zǒu lù.
(Woh she-hwahn dzow-loo) 我喜欢走路。

Is it too far to walk?
Zǒu lù qù tài yuǎn le ma?
(Dzow loo chwee tie ywahn-ler ma) 走路去太远了吗?

Can I walk there from the hotel?
Wǒ néng cóng lǚguǎn zǒu qù ma? 我能从旅馆走去吗?
(Woh nerng tsohng lwee-gwahn dzow chwee mah)

Hotel Lǚguǎn *(Lwee-gwahn)* 旅馆; Fàndiàn *(Fahn-dee-an)* 饭店

reservations	*yùdìng (yuu-deeng)* 预定
reservations desk	*yùdìng chù (yuu-deeng choo)* 预定处
hotel concierge	*jiēdài yuán (jeh-die-ywahn)* 接待员
service fee	*fúwùfèi (foo-woo fay)* 服务费
lobby datang	*dà táng (da-tahng)* 大堂
check in	*rùzhù (roo-joo)* 入住
check out	*tuìfáng (tway-fahng)* 退房
cashier	*chūnà (choo-nah)* 出纳
room key	*yàoshi (yee-ow shr)* 钥匙
room number	*fángjiān hàomǎ (fahng-jee-an how-mah)* 房间号码
single room	*dānrén fáng (dahn-wren fahng)* 单人房
double room	*shuāngrén fáng (shwahng-wren fahng)* 双人房
twin room	*shuāngchuáng fáng (shwahng chwang fahng)* 双床房
suite	*tàofáng (tao fahng)* 套房
airconditioning	*kōngtiáo (kohng-tee-ow)* 空调
laundry bag	*xǐyī dài (she-ee die)* 洗衣袋
laundry form	*xǐyī dān (she-ee dahn)* 洗衣单
morning call service	*jiàoxǐng fúwù (jee-ow sheeng foo-woo)* 叫醒服务
"Do not disturb"	*qǐng wù dǎrǎo (cheeng woo dah-rao)* 请勿打扰
"Make up room"	*qǐng dǎsǎo (cheeng dah-sao)* 请打扫

I have / don't have a reservation.
Wǒ yǐjīng / méiyǒu yùdìng le fángjiān.
(Woh ee-jeeng/may you yuu-deeng-ler fahng-jee-an)
我已经／没有预定了房间。

Do you have any vacancies?
Yǒu kòng fángjiān ma?
(You kohng fahng-jee-an mah) 有空房间吗?

I will be staying for two nights.
Wǒ yào zhù liǎng wǎn.
(Woh yow joo lee-ahng wang) 我要住两晚。

I would like it for two nights.
Wǒ xiǎng zhù liǎng yè.
(Woh she-ahng joo lee-ahng yeh) 我想要住两夜。

I would like a room with a view.
Wǒ yào hǎo fēngjǐng de fáng. 我要好风景的房。
(Woh yee-aw how ferng jeeng der fahng)

How much is the room rate?
Fáng fèi duōshao qián?
(Fahng fay dwoh-shou chee-an) 房费多少钱?

What time is breakfast?
Jǐdiǎn chī zǎocān?
(Jee-dee-an chr dzow-fahn) 几点吃早餐?

Do you have English language newspapers?
Nǐmen zhè yǒu méiyǒu Yīngwén bàozhǐ?
(Nee-mern jr you may you Eeng-wern bow-jr)
你们这有没有英文报纸?

I've lost my key.
Wǒ diū le yàoshi.
(Woh deo ler yow-shr) 我丢了钥匙。

What time is check out?
Shénme shíjiān tuìfáng?
(Shern-mo shr-jee-an tway-fahng) 什么时间退房？

Is there a service fee?
Yǒu fúwùfèi ma?
(You foo-woo fay mah) 有服务费吗？

breakfast   *zǎocān (zow tsahn)* 早餐

Most Chinese hotels and some motels / hostels offer free breakfast and / or Internet during stay. Be sure to check with the front desk.

Is the breakfast included (in the room price)?
Fáng jià bāokuò zǎocān ma?
(Fahng-jee-ah bow kway zow-tsahn mah)
房价包括早餐吗？

Is free Internet included (in the room price)?
Fáng jià bāokuò miǎnfèi shàngwǎng ma?
(Fahng-jee-ah bow kway mee-an-fay shahng-wahng mah) 房价包括免费上网吗？

Room Service *Kèfáng yòngcān fúwùbù*

(Ker-fahng yohng-tsahn foo-woo-boo) 客房用餐服务部

I would like to order breakfast.
Wǒ xiǎng dìng zǎocān.
(Woh she-ahng deeng dzow-tsahn) 我想订早餐。

Do you serve (have) Western food?
Yǒu Xīcān ma? (You she tsahn mah) 有西餐吗?

Do you have Japanese food?
Yǒu Rìběn liàolǐ ma?
(You ree-bern lee-ow-lee mah) 有日本料理吗?

Please bring me some scrambled eggs and toast.
Qǐng ná chǎo jīdàn hé miànbāo gěi wǒ.
(Cheeng nah chow jee-dahn her kow mee-an-bow gay woh) 请拿炒鸡蛋和面包给我。

Numbers *Hàomǎ* *(How-oh-mah)* 号码

The Cardinal Numbers

0	*líng (leeng)* 零
1	*yī (ee)** 一
2	*èr (urr)* 二; also *liǎng (lee-ahng)* 两
3	*sān (sahn)* 三
4	*sì (suh)* 四
5	*wǔ (woo)* 五
6	*liù (leo)* 六
7	*qī (chee)* 七
8	*bā (bah)* 八

9 *jiǔ (jeo)* 九
10 *shí (shr)* 十

*Sometimes, for easier pronunciation, the number 1 can be pronounced *yāo* (*yow*) instead of *yī* (*yee*).

From 10 on, the numbers are combinations of the first ten numbers. Eleven is 10 and 1, 12 is 10 and 2, etc. Twenty is 2-10; 30 is 3-10, and so on.

11 *shíyī (shr-ee)* 十一
12 *shíèr (shr-urr)* 十二
13 *shísān (shr-sahn)* 十三
14 *shísì (shr-suh)* 十四
15 *shíwǔ (shr-woo)* 十五
16 *shíliù (shr-leo)* 十六
17 *shíqī (shr-chee)* 十七
18 *shíbā (shr-bah)* 十八
19 *shíjiǔ (shr-jeo)* 十九
20 *èrshí (urr-shr)* 二十
...
30 *sānshí (sahn-shr)* 三十
40 *sìshí (suh-shr)* 四十
50 *wǔshí (woo-shr)* 五十
60 *liùshí (leo-shr)* 六十
70 *qīshí (chee-shr)* 七十
80 *bāshí (bah-shr)* 八十
90 *jiǔshí (jeo-shr)* 九十
100 *yībǎi (ee-by)** 一百

**bǎi* (*by*) is the designator for 100.

From 100 on, the numbers are combinations of the 100 + 0
(zero) + the ten numbers. So, 101 is 100 + 0 +1, and so
on, as follows:

101	*yībǎi líng yī (ee-by-leeng-ee)* 一百零一	
102	*yībǎi líng èr (ee-by-leeng-urr)* 一百零二	
103	*yībǎi líng sān (ee-by-leeng-sahn)* 一百零三	
104	*yībǎi líng sì (ee-by-leeng-suh)* 一百零四	
105	*yībǎi líng wǔ (ee-by-leeng-woo)* 一百零五	
106	*yībǎi líng liù (ee-by-leeng-leo)* 一百零六	
107	*yībǎi líng qī (ee-by-leeng-chee)* 一百零七	
108	*yībǎi líng bā (ee-by-leeng-bah)* 一百零八	
109	*yībǎi líng jiǔ (ee-by-leeng-jeo)* 一百零九	
110	*yībǎi yī shí (ee-by-yee-suhr)* 一百一十	
120	*yībǎi èrshí (ee-by-urr-shr)* 一百二十	
130	*yībǎi sānshí (ee-by-sahn-shr)* 一百三十	
140	*yībǎi sìshí (ee-by-suh-shr)* 一百四十	
150	*yībǎi wǔshí (ee-by-woo-shr)* 一百五十	
175	*yībǎi qīshí wǔ (ee-by-chee-shr-woo)* 一百七十五	
200	*èrbǎi (urr-by)* 二百	
201	*èrbǎi líng yī (urr-by-leeng-ee)* 二百零一	
300	*sānbǎi (sahn-by)* 三百	
400	*sìbǎi (suh-by)* 四百	
500	*wǔbǎi (woo-by)* 五百	
600	*liùbǎi (leo-by)* 六百	
700	*qībǎi (chee-by)* 七百	
800	*bābǎi (bah-by)* 八百	
900	*jiǔbǎi (jeo-by)* 九百	
1,000	*yīqiān* (ee-chee-an)* 一千	

*Qiān (chee-an) is the designator for 1,000.

1,500	*yīqiān wǔbǎi* *(ee-chee-an-woo-by)* 一千五百
2,000	*liǎngqiān (lee-ahng-chee-an)* 两千
2,700	*liǎngqiān qībǎi* *(lee-ahng-chee-an-chee-by)* 两千七百
10,000	*yīwàn* (ee-wahn)* 一万

***Wàn** *(wahn)* is the designator for 10,000 – this is the term used in Chinese for 10,000 (ten thousand), so non-speaking Chinese need to get used to this term.

11,000	*yīwàn yīqiān* *(ee-wahn-ee-chee-an)* 一万一千
12,000	*yīwàn liǎngqiān* *(ee-wahn-leeng-chee-an)* 一万两千
15,000	*yīwàn wǔqiān* *(ee-wahn-woo-chee-an)* 一万五千
100,000	*shíwàn (shr-wahn)* 十万
150,000	*shíwǔwàn (shr-woo-wahn)* 十五万
200,000	*èrshíwàn (urr-shr-wahn)* 二十万
300,000	*sānshíwàn (sahn-shr-wahn)* 三十万
500,000	*wǔshíwàn (woo-shr-wahn)* 五十万
1,000,000	*yībǎiwàn (ee-by-wahn)* 一百万

The Ordinal Numbers

The ordinal numbers are created by adding the prefix *dì (dee)* to the cardinal numbers.

1st	*dìyī (dee-ee)* 第一
2nd	*dìèr (dee-urr)* 第二
3rd	*dìsān (dee-sahn)* 第三

4th	*dìsì (dee-suh)*	第四
5th	*dìwǔ (dee-woo)*	第五
6th	*dìliù (dee-leo)*	第六
7th	*dìqī (dee-chee)*	第七
8th	*dìbā (dee-bah)*	第八
9th	*dìjiǔ (dee-jeo)*	第九
10th	*dìshí (dee-shr)*	第十
and so on …		
20th	*dìèrshí (dee-urr-shr)*	第二十
30th	*dìsānshí (dee-sahn-shr)*	第三十
50th	*dìwǔshí (dee-woo-shr)*	第五十
one half	*yībàn (ee-bahn)*	一半
one quarter	*sìfēnzhīyī (suh fern jr ee)*	四分之一

43 Counting Things *Dōngxi (Dohng-she)* 东西

The Chinese language uses special indicators, or "measure words," for counting things, based on what they are—people, flat things, round things, animals, fish, etc. There are over a dozen such terms, so keeping them straight, and using them properly, can be a problem for the beginner.

However, the most common of these indicators, *gè (guh)* 个, can be used when you are uncertain about which one to use. The measure words go between the numbers and the nouns they apply to. Here is a list of the most common ones:

Counting

• books: *běn (bern)* 本

one book
yī běn shū (ee-bern shoo) 一本书

- the number of times something occurs:
  cì (tsu) 次
- trees: *kē (ker)* 棵
- buildings and houses: *suǒ (swoh)* 所
- large, long, slender objects such as telephone cables: *tiáo (tee-ow)* 条
- small, round objects like pencils and sticks: *zhī (jr)* 支
- flat things like pieces of paper: *zhāng (jahng)* 张

two sheets of paper
liǎng zhāng zhǐ (lee-ahng-jahng jr) 两张纸

- bowls and things that come in bowls:
  wǎn (wahn) 碗
- bottles and bottled things: *píng (peeng)* 瓶

two bottles of beer
liǎngpíng píjiǔ (lee-ahng-peeng pee-jeo) 两瓶啤酒

- money: *kuài (kwie)* 块
- glasses of water, etc: *bēi (bay)* 杯

three glasses of water
sānbēi shuǐ (sahn-bay shway) 三杯水

I have three books.
Wǒ yǒu sānběn shū.
(Woh you sahn-ben shoo) 我有三本书。

Please give me one sheet of paper.
Qǐng gěi wǒ yīzhāng zhǐ.
(Cheeng gay woh ee-jahng jr) 请给我一张纸。

Two glasses of water, please.
Qǐng gěi liǎngbēi shuǐ.
(Cheeng gay lee-ahng-bay shway) 请给两杯水。

One hamburger, please.
Qǐng gěi yīge hànbǎo bāo. 请给一个汉堡包。
(Cheeng gay ee-guh hahn-bow-bow)

44   Counting People *Rén* (wren) 人

person/people	*rén* (wren-meen) 人
1 person	*yīge rén* (ee-guh wren) 一个人
2 persons	*liǎngge rén* 两个人
	(lee-ahng-guh wren)
3 persons	*sānge rén* (sahn-ge wren) 三个人
4 persons	*sìge rén* (suh-guh wren) 四个人
5 persons	*wǔge rén* (woo-guh wren) 五个人
6 persons	*liùge rén* (leo-guh wren) 六个人
7 persons	*qīge rén* (chee-guh wren) 七个人
8 persons	*bāge rén* (bah-guh wren) 八个人
9 persons	*jiǔge rén* (jeo-guh wren) 九个人
10 people	*shíge rén* (shr-guh wren) 十个人

*位 *wèi* (way) is used for counting person / people in polite language. Example: 一位老师 *yīwèi lǎoshī* (yee-way lao-shr) (a teacher) instead of 一个老师 *yīge lǎoshī* (yee-guh lao-shr).

Time *Diǎn* *(Dee-an)* 点

Telling time in Chinese is a combination of the appropriate number, plus *diǎn* *(dee-an)*, which means something like "point of time." In this usage it is the equivalent of the English "o'clock."

time (of day)	*shíjiān* *(shr-jee-an)* 时间
hour	*xiǎoshí* *(shee-ow-shr)* 小时
half an hour	*bàn xiǎoshí* *(bahn-shee-ow-shr)* 半小时
minute	*fēn* *(fern)* 分
a.m.	*shàngwǔ* *(shahng-woo)* 上午
p.m.	*xiàwǔ* *(shee-ah-woo)* 下午

In China the 24-hour day is divided into four periods:

midnight to 6 a.m. (early morning)	*qīngzǎo* *(cheeng-zow)* 清早
6 a.m. to noon (morning)	*zǎoshang* *(zow-shahng)* 早上
noon to 6 p.m. (afternoon)	*xiàwǔ* *(shee-ah-woo)* 下午
6 p.m. to midnight (evening)	*wǎnshang* *(wahn-shahng)* 晚上

In designating the time period as well as the hour, both words precede the hour, as in the following examples.

1 a.m.	*qīngzǎo yī diǎn* *(cheeng-zow ee dee-an)* 清早一点

8 a.m.	*zǎoshang bā diǎn* (zow-shahng bah dee-an) 早上八点	
1 p.m.	*xiàwǔ yī diǎn* (shee-ah-woo ee dee-an) 下午一点	
8 p.m.	*wǎnshang bā diǎn* 晚上八点 (wahn-shahng bah dee-an)	
what time?	*jǐdiǎn?* (jee dee-an) 几点?	
at / in	*zài* (zigh) 在	
early	*zǎo* (zow) 早	
late	*wǎn* (wahn) 晚	
on time	*zhǔnshí* (ju-wun-shr) 准时	
in the morning	*zài zǎoshang* (zigh zow-shahng) 在早上	
in the afternoon	*zài xiàwǔ* (zigh shee-ah-woo) 在下午	
in the evening	*zài wǎnshang* (zigh wahn-shahng) 在晚上	
1 o'clock	*yī diǎn* (ee dee-an) 一点	
1 a.m.	*zǎoshang yī diǎn* (zow-shahng ee-dee-an) 早上一点	
1:10	*yī diǎn shí fēn* (ee dee-an shr fern) 一点十分	
1:30	*yī diǎn bàn* (ee dee-an bahn) 一点半	
2 o'clock	*liǎng diǎn* (lee-ahng dee-an) 两点	
3 o'clock	*sān diǎn* (sahn dee-an) 三点	
2 a.m.	*zǎoshang liǎng diǎn* 早上两点 (zow-shahng lee-ahng dee-an)	
2 p.m.	*xiàwǔ liǎng diǎn* 下午两点 (shee-ah-woo lee-ahng dee-an)	
2:30	*liǎng diǎn bàn* (lee-ahng dee-an bahn)	

3.15	*sān diǎn shíwǔ fēn / sān diǎn yī kè* *(sahn dee-an shr-woo-fern/yee ker)* 三点十五分／三点一刻
3:30	*sān diǎn bàn* *(sahn dee-an bahn)* 三点半
4 o'clock	*sì diǎn (suh dee-an)* 四点
5 o'clock	*wǔ diǎn (woo dee-an)* 五点
6 o'clock	*liù diǎn (leo dee-an)* 六点
7 o'clock	*qī diǎn (chee dee-an)* 七点
8 o'lock	*bā diǎn (bah dee-an)* 八点
9 o'clock	*jiǔ diǎn (jeo dee-an)* 九点
10 o'clock	*shí diǎn (shr dee-an)* 十点
11 o'clock	*shíyī diǎn (shr-ee dee-an)* 十一点
12 o'clock	*shíèr diǎn (shr-urr dee-an)* 十二点

What time is it (now)?
Jǐdiǎn le? (Jee dee-an ler) 几点了？

It is 6:30.
Liù diǎn sānshí / liù diǎn bàn.
(Leo dee-an sahn-shr / bahn) 六点三十／六点半。

It is 12:30
Shí èr diǎn sānshí / shí èr diǎn bàn.
(Shr-urr dee-an sahn-shr / bahn)
十二点三十／十二点半。

What time are we leaving?
Wǒmen shénme shíjiān zǒu?
(Woh-mern shern-mo shr-jee-an zoe) 我们什么时间走？

What time does the bus leave?
Gōnggòng qìchē jǐdiǎn chūfā?
(Gohng-gohng chee-cher jee-dee-an chuu-fah)
公共汽车几点出发?

What time is breakfast / lunch / dinner?
Zǎocān / wǔcān / wǎncān shì jǐdiǎn?
(Zow-tsahn/wuu-tsahn/wahn-tsahn shr jee dee-an)
早餐／午餐／晚餐 是几点?

One moment, please.
Qǐng děng yī děng.
(Cheeng derng ee derng) 请等一等。

What time does the museum open?
Bówùguǎn jǐdiǎn kāimén? 博物馆几点开门?
(Boh-woo-gwahn jee-dee-an kigh-mern)

What time does the theater open?
Jùchǎng jǐdiǎn kāimén?
(Jwee-chahng jee-dee-an kigh-mern) 剧场几点开门?

What time does the play / film start?
Huàjù / diànyǐng jǐdiǎn kāishǐ?
(Hwah-jwee / dee-an-yeeng jee-dee-an kigh shr)
话剧／电影 几点开始?

46 Days *Tiān* (Tee-an) 天

The days of the week, from Monday through Saturday, consist of the "day designator" *xīngqī* (sheeng-chee) plus the numbers one through six. Sunday consists of the "day designator" plus *tiān* (tee-an), the word for "day."

Monday	*xīngqīyī* (Sheeng-chee-ee) 星期一
Tuesday	*xīngqīèr* (Sheeng-chee-urr) 星期二
Wednesday	*xīngqīsān* (Sheeng-chee-sahn) 星期三
Thursday	*xīngqīsì* (Sheeng-chee-suh) 星期四
Friday	*xīngqīwǔ* (Sheeng-chee-woo) 星期五
Saturday	*xīngqīliù* (Sheeng-chee-leo) 星期六
Sunday	*xīngqītiān* (Sheeng-chee-tee-an) 星期天
today	*jīntiān* (jeen-tee-an) 今天

What day is today?
Jīntiān shì xīngqī jǐ?
(Jeen-tee-an shr Sheeng-chee jee) 今天是星期几?

Today is Monday.
Jīntiān shì xīngqīyī.
(Jeen-tee-an shr Sheeng-chee-ee) 今天是星期一。

every day	*měitiān* (may-tee-an) 每天
tomorrow	*míngtiān* (meeng-tee-an) 明天
tomorrow morning	*míngtiān shàngwǔ* 明天上午 (meeng-tee-an shahng-woo)
tomorrow afternoon	*míngtiān xiàwǔ* 明天下午 (meeng-tee-an she-ah-woo)
this morning	*jīntiān zǎoshang* 今天早上 (jeen-tee-an zow-shahng)
this afternoon	*jīntiān xiàwǔ* 今天下午 (jeen-tee-an she-ah-woo)
day after tomorrow	*hòutiān* (hoe tee-an) 后天
yesterday	*zuótiān* (zwoh-tee-an) 昨天

day before yesterday	*qiántiān (chee-an tee-an)*	前天
in the morning	*zài zǎoshang (zigh zow-shahng)*	在早上
in the afternoon	*zài xiàwǔ (zigh she-ah-woo)*	在下午
in the evening	*zia wǎnshang (zigh wahn-shahng)*	在晚上
last night	*zuótiān wǎnshang (zwoh-tee-an wahn-shahng)*	昨天晚上
early	*zǎo (zow)*	早
late	*wǎn (wahn)*	晚
on time	*zhǔnshí (joon-shr)*	准时

Counting Days

1 day	*yī tiān (ee tee-an)*	一天
2 days	*liǎng tiān (lee-ahng tee-an)*	两天
3 days	*sān tiān (sahn tee-an)*	三天
4 days	*sì tiān (suh tee-an)*	四天
5 days	*wǔ tiān (woo tee-an)*	五天
6 days	*liù tiān (leo tee-an)*	六天
7 days	*qī tiān (chee tee-an)*	七天
8 days	*bā tiān (bah tee-an)*	八天
9 days	*jiǔ tiān (jeo tee-an)*	九天
10 days	*shí tiān (shr tee-an)*	十天
21 days	*èrshíyī tiān (urr-shr-ee tee-an)*	二十一天

Note: When counting days, there is no need for a measure word.

Weeks *Xīngqī* (Sheen-chee) 星期

this week	*zhège xīngqī*
	(jay-guh sheeng-chee) 这个星期
last week	*shànggè xīngqī*
	(shahng-guh sheeng-chee) 上个星期
next week	*xiàgè xīngqī*
	(she-ah-guh sheeng-chee) 下个星期
weekend	*zhōumò* (joe-mwo) 周末
week after next	*xià xiàgè xīngqī* 下下个星期
	(she-ah-shah-guh sheeng-chee)

Counting Weeks

1 week	*yī xīngqī* (ee sheeng-chee) 一星期
2 weeks	*èr xīngqī* (urr sheeng-chee) 二星期
3 weeks	*sānxīng qī* (sahn sheeng-chee) 三星期
4 weeks	*sì xīngqī* (suh sheeng-chee) 四星期
5 weeks	*wǔ xīngqī* (woo sheeng-chee) 五星期
6 weeks	*liù xīngqī* (leo sheeng-chee) 六星期
7 weeks	*qī xīngqī* (chee sheeng-chee) 七星期
8 weeks	*bā xīngqī* (bah sheeng-chee) 八星期

I will be in China for two weeks.

Wǒ jiāng zài Zhōngguó dài liǎng ge xīngqī.
(Woh jee-ahng zigh Johng-gwoh die lee-ahng-guh sheeng-chee) 我将在中国待两个星期。

Months *Yuè (Yuu-eh)* 月

The Chinese word for month is **yuè** *(yuu-eh)*. **Yuè** is used when naming or listing the months, and **rì** *(ree)* is used when giving dates. The names of the months consist of the appropriate number plus **yuè**—in other words, **yī** *(one)* plus **yuè** *(month)* equals January.

January	*Yīyuè (Ee-yuu-eh)* 一月
February	*Èryuè (Urr-yuu-eh)* 二月
March	*Sānyuè (Sahn-yuu-eh)* 三月
April	*Sìyuè (Suh-yuu-eh)* 四月
May	*Wǔyuè (Woo-yuu-eh)* 五月
June	*Liùyuè (Leo-yuu-eh)* 六月
July	*Qīyuè (Chee-yuu-eh)* 七月
August	*Bāyuè (Bah-yuu-eh)* 八月
September	*Jiǔyuè (Jeo-yuu-eh)* 九月
October	*Shíyuè (Shr-yuu-eh)* 十月
November	*Shíyīyuè (Shr-ee-yuu-eh)* 十一月
December	*Shíèryuè (Shr-urr-yuu-eh)* 十二月
this month	*zhègè yuè (jay-guh yuu-eh)* 这个月
next month	*xiàgè yuè (shee-ah-guh yuu-eh)* 下个月
last month	*shànggè yuè (shahng-guh yuu-eh)* 上个月
month after next	*xià xiàgè yuè (shee-ah-shee-ah-guh yuu-eh)* 下下个月
monthly	*měi gè yuè (may-guh yuu-eh)* 每个月

To enumerate months, add the prefix **gè** *(guh)* to **yuè**, the word for month, and put the appropriate number in front of the word:

1 month	*yī gè yuè* (ee guh-yuu-eh)	一个月
2 months	*liǎng gè yuè* (lee-ahng-guh-yuu-eh)	两个月
5 months	*wǔ gè yuè* (woo guh-yuu-eh)	五个月
6 months	*liù gè yuè* (leo guh-yuu-eh)	六个月
12 months	*shíèr gè yuè* (shr-urr guh-yuu-eh)	十二个月
every month	*měi gè yuè* (may-guh yuu-eh)	每个月
a few months	*jǐ gè yuè* (jee-guh yuu-eh)	几个月

Years *Nián* (Nee-an) 年

this year	*jīnnián* (jeen nee-an)	今年
next year	*míngnián* (meeng nee-an)	明年
last year	*qùnián* (chwee nee-an)	去年
every year	*měi nián* (may nee-an)	每年
one year	*yī nián* (ee nee-an)	一年
two years	*liǎng nián* (lee-ahng nee-an)	两年
three years	*sān nián* (sahn nee-an)	三年
four years	*sì nián* (suh nee-an)	四年
five years	*wǔ nián* (woo nee-an)	五年
Happy New Year!	*Xīn Nián Hǎo!* (Sheen Nee-an How)	新年好!
New Year's Day	*Yuándàn* (Ywahn Dahn)	元旦

Drink *Hē* (Huh) 喝

beverage	*yǐnliào* (een-lee-ow)	饮料
coffee	*kāfēi* (kah-fay)	咖啡
milk	*niúnǎi* (new-nigh)	牛奶
tea	*chá* (chah)	茶
water	*shuǐ* (shway)	水
mineral water	*kuàngquán shuǐ* (kwahng-chwahn shway)	矿泉水
ice	*bīng* (beeng)	冰
soya-bean milk	*dòujiāng* (doe-jee-ahng)	豆浆
tomato juice	*fānqié zhī* (fahn-chee-eh jr)	番茄汁
coconut milk	*yēzi zhī* (yeh-dzu jr)	椰子汁
grapefruit juice	*xīyòu zhī* (she-yuu jr)	西柚汁
vegetable juice	*shūcài zhī* (shoo-tsigh jr)	蔬菜汁
ginger ale	*jiāngzhī qìshuǐ* (jee-ahng-jr chee-shway)	姜汁汽水
sarsaparilla	*shāshì* (shah-shr)	沙士
coco-cola (coke)	*kěkǒu kělè* (ker-koe ker-ler)	可口可乐
lemon tea	*níngméng chá* (neeng-merng)	柠檬茶
soda water	*sūdá shuǐ* (soo-dah shway)	苏打水
condensed milk	*liànrǔ* (lee-an-roo)	炼乳
cocoa	*kěkě* (ker-ker)	可可
ovaltine	*Āhuàtián* (ah-hwa tee-an)	阿华田
yakult	*Yǎnglèduō* (yahng-ler-dwoh)	养乐多

ice-cream	*xuěgāo (she-eh-gow)* 雪糕
	bīngqílín (been-qi-lee) 冰淇淋
milk-shake	*nǎixī (nigh-she)* 奶昔

I'm thirsty.
Wǒ kě le. (Woh ker ler) 我渴了。

I'd like a beverage.
Wǒ xiǎng diǎn yǐnliào.
(Woh shee-ahng dee-an een-lee-ow) 我想点饮料。

What do you want to drink?
Nǐ xiǎng hē shénme?
(Nee she-ahng her shern-mo) 你想喝什么?

I'll have coffee, please.
Qǐng gěi wǒ kāfēi.
(Cheeng gay woh kah-fay) 请给我咖啡。

I'll have black coffee, please.
Qǐng gěi wǒ hēi kāfēi.
(Cheeng gay woh-hay kah-fay) 请给我黑咖啡。

More coffee, please.
Qǐng duō lái kāfēi.
(Cheeng dwoh lie kah-fay) 请多来咖啡。

I'll have green tea, please
Qǐng lái yībēi lùchá.
(Cheeng lie ee bay lwee-chah) 请来 一杯绿茶。

Tea with milk, please.
Qǐng lái yībēi hóngchá jiā niúnǎi.
(Cheeng lie ee-bay hohng-chah jah new-nigh)
请来一杯红茶加牛奶。

I'll have tea with lemon, please.
Qǐng lái yībēi níngméng chá. 请来一杯柠檬茶。
(Cheeng lie ee bay neen-merng chah)

More tea, please.
Qǐng duō lái chá.(Cheeng dwoh lie char) 请多来茶。

A glass of milk, please.
Qǐng lái yībēi niúnǎi.
(Cheeng lie ee-bay new-nigh) 请来一杯牛奶。

Mineral water, please.
Qǐng lái yībēi kuàngquánshuǐ. 请来一杯矿泉水。
(Cheeng lie ee-bay kwahng-chwahn shway)

May I have a straw (for my drink)?
Qǐng gěi wǒ xīguǎn.
(Cheeng gay woh she-gwahn) 请给我吸管。

---

51   **Bar** *Jiǔbā* *(Jew-bah)* 酒吧

beer	*píjiǔ (pee-jew)* 啤酒	
draft beer	*shēng pí (sherng pee)* 生啤	
black beer	*hēi píjiǔ (hay pee-jew)* 黑啤酒	
wine	*pútaojiǔ (poo-tao-jew)* 葡萄酒	
red wine	*hóng pútaojiǔ*	
	(hohng poo-tao-jew) 红葡萄酒	

white wine	*bái pútaojiǔ*
	(*bigh poo-tao jew*) 白葡萄酒
martini	*Mǎdīngní*
	(*mah-deen-nee*) 马丁尼
tea set	*chájù* (*chah-jwee*) 茶具
whisky with	*Wēishìjì jiā sūdá* 威士忌加苏达
soda	(*way-shr-jee jah soo-dah*)
whisky with	*Wēishìjì jiā shuǐ*
water	(*way-shr-jee jah shway*) 威士忌加水

Let's go get a drink.
Wǒmen qù hē jiǔ. (*Woh-mern chwee her jew*)
我们去喝酒。

A glass of red wine.
Yībēi hóng pútaojiǔ.
(*Ee bay hohng poo-tao-jew*) 一杯红葡萄酒。

Two glasses of white wine.
Liǎngbēi bái pútaojiǔ.
(*Lee-ahng bay bigh poo-tao-jew*) 两杯白葡萄酒。

A bottle of beer, please.
Qǐng lái yīpíng píjiǔ.
(*Cheeng lie ee ping pee-jew*) 请来一瓶啤酒。

Two bottles of beer, please.
Qǐng lái liǎngpíng píjiǔ.
(*Cheeng lie lee-ahng ping pee-jew*) 请来两瓶啤酒。

A glass of beer, please.
Qǐng lái yībēi píjiǔ.
(*Cheeng lie ee bay pee-jew*) 请来一杯啤酒。

Draft beer, please.
Qǐng lái yībēi shēng píjiǔ.
(Cheeng lie ee-bay sherng pee-jew) 请来一杯生啤酒。

Two maotai, please.
Qǐng lái liǎngbēi máo tái.
(Cheeng lie lee-ahng bay mao-tie) 请来两杯茅台。

The bill, please.
Qǐng jiézhàng / mǎidān.
(Cheeng jee-eh-jahng/ my-dahn) 请结帐／买单。

---

52 | Eat *Chī* (Chr) 吃

food	*fàn* (fahn) 饭 / *cān* (tsahn) 餐	
Chinese food	*Zhōngcān (Johng-tsahn)* 中餐	
Western food	*Xīcān (She tsahn)* 西餐	
restaurant	*fànguǎn* (fahn-gwahn) 饭馆 / *cānguǎn* (tsahn gwahn) 餐馆	
hotel restaurant	*fàndiàn* (fahn dee-an) 饭店	
dining room	*cāntīng* (tsahn teeng) 餐厅	
coffee shop	*kāfēi tīng* (kah-fay teeng) 咖啡厅	
American-style breakfast	*Měiguó zǎocān* 美国早餐 (May-gwoh zow-fahn)	
menu	*càidān* (tsigh-dahn) 菜单	
rice (cooked)	*mǐfàn* (me-fahn) 米饭	

I'm hungry.
Wǒ è le. *(Woh uh-ler)* 我饿了。

What do you want to eat?
Nǐ xiǎng chī shénme?
(Nee she-ahng chr shern-mo) 你想吃什么?

Where shall we go to eat?
Wǒmen qù nǎlǐ chī?
(Woh-mern chwee nah-lee chr) 我们去哪里吃?

What time do we eat?
Wǒmen shénme shíjiān chīfàn?
(Woh-mern shern-mo shr jee-an chr-fahn)
我们什么时间吃饭?

Let's go eat.
Wǒmen qù chīfàn. *(Woh-mern chwee chr-fahn)*
我们去吃饭。

I like Chinese food.
Wǒ xǐhuan Zhōngcān. *(Woh she-hwahn Johng tsahn)*
我喜欢中餐。

A table for two, please.
Liǎng wèi. *(lee-ahng way)* 两位。

A menu (or menus), please.
Qǐng ná càidān. *(Cheeng na tsigh dahn)* 请拿菜单。

What is that?
Nà shì shénme?
(Nay she shern-mo) 那是什么?

I want that.
Wǒ yào nà ge. *(Woh yee-ow nay-guh)* 我要那个。

Please give me ____.
Qǐng gěi wǒ ____. *(Cheeng gay woh ____)*
请给我 ____。

Please bring me ____.
Qǐng sòng ____ lái .
(Cheeng sohng ____ lie) 请送 ____ 来。

I would like _____.
Wǒ xiǎng yào _____.
(Woh she-ahng yee-ow _____) 我想要 _____。

More butter, please.
Qǐng duō lái huángyóu.
(Cheeng dwoh lie hwahng-you) 请多来黄油。

Just a little, please.
Jiù yīdiǎn diǎn.
(Jew ee-dee-an-urr dee-an-urr) 就一点点。

Is that enough?
Nà xiē gòu le ma? *(Nah shay go-ler mah)* 那些够了吗?

Please give me a little more.
Qǐng gěi wǒ duō yīdiǎn.
(Cheeng gay woh dwoh ee-dee-an) 请给我多一点。

That's enough!
Nà xiē gòu le! *(Nah shay go-ler)* 那些够了!

That's too much!
Nà xiē tài duō le!
(Nah shay tie dwoh-ler) 那些太多了!

I can't eat all of this!
Wǒ bùnéng chī wán suǒ yǒu de! 我不能吃完所有的!
(Woh boo nerng chr wahn swoh you-der)

53 Dim Sum* *Diǎnxin* *(Dee-an Sheen)* 点心

*This famous Cantonese dish (known virtually around the world) is called *diǎnxin (dee-an sheen)* in Mandarin, the national language.

egg tart	*dàn tà (dahn tah)* 蛋挞
sweet cream bun	*nǎi huáng bāo* *(nigh-hwahng bow)* 奶皇包
preserved egg and pork porridge	*pídàn shòuròu zhōu* *(pee-dahn show-roe dzow)* 皮蛋瘦肉粥
crispy fried squid	*yóuyú sū* *(you-yuu soo)* 鱿鱼酥
turnip cake	*luóbo gāo* *(lwaw-bwo gow)* 萝卜糕
steamed dumplings	*xiā jiǎo (she-ah jee-ow)* 虾饺
char siu bao (BBQed pork bun)	*chāshāo bāo* *(tsah-shou bow)* 叉烧包
Pheonix (chicken) Claws	*fèng zhuǎ (ferng jwah)* 凤爪
lotus leaf rice	*nuòmǐ jī (nwoh-me jee)* 糯米鸡

We want to eat dim sum.
Wǒmen yào chī diǎnxin.
(Woh-mern yee-ow chr dee-an sheen) 我们要吃点心。

I want to go to a dim sum restaurant.
Wǒ yào qù diǎnxin fànguǎn.
(Woh yow chwee dee-an sheen fahn-gwahn)
我要去点心饭馆。

I'm full!
Wǒ bǎo le! (Woh bow-ler) 我饱了!

Peking Duck *Běijīng Kǎoyā* (Bay-jeeng Kow-yah) 北京烤鸭

I'd like to have Peking Duck.
Wǒ yào chī Běijīng kǎoyā.
(Woh yee-ow chr Bay-jeeng Kow-yah)
我要吃北京烤鸭。

I want to go to a Beijing Duck restaurant.
Wǒ xiǎng qù yī gè Běijīng kǎoyā guǎn.
(Woh she-ahng chwee ee-guh Bay-jeen kow-yah gwahn) 我想去一个北京烤鸭馆。

Is it very expensive?
Hěn guì ma? (Hern gwee mah) 很贵吗?

I'd like to make reservations for dinner this evening.
Wǒ yào dìng jīntiān de wǎnfàn.
(Woh yee-ow deeng jeen-tee-an der wahn-fahn)
我要订今天的晚饭。

There will be three of us.
Wǒmen yǒu sān wèi. (Woh-mern you sahn-wei)
我们有三位。

Like / Don't Like *Xǐhuan* *(She-hwahn)* 喜欢 / *Bù Xǐhuan* *(Boo she-hwahn)* 不喜欢

I like it.
Xǐhuan. (She-hwahn) 喜欢。

I don't like it.
Bù xǐhuan. (Boo she-hwahn) 不喜欢。

I like Chinese food.
Xǐhuan Zhōngcān.
(she-hwahn johng tsahn) 喜欢中餐。

I'd like Western food.
Wǒ xiǎng yào Xīcān.
(Woh she-ahng yee-ow She tsigh) 我想要西餐。

It's delicious.
Hǎochī. (How chr-der) 好吃。

It tastes good.
Kěkǒu. (Ker-koh) 可口。

I don't like to eat Chinese food every day.
Bù xǐhuan měi tiān chī Zhōngcān.
(Boo she-hwahn may-tee-an cheen Johng tsahn)
不喜欢每天吃中餐。

Shanghai xiaolongbao (steamed bun)	*Shànghǎi xiǎolóngbāo* *(shahng-hi she-ow-lohng bow)* 上海小笼包
sweet and sour pork	*tángcù lǐ jǐ* *(tahng tsu lee jee)* 糖醋里脊

dumplings	*jiǎozi (jee-ow joo)* 饺子
wontons	*húntún (hoon toon)* 馄饨
Chinese fried breadstick	*yóutiáo (you tee-ow)* 油条
Nanjing salted duck	*yánshuǐ yā (yahn-shway yah)* 盐水鸭
meatballs	*shīzi tóu (shr-dzu toe)* 狮子头
sweet and sour carp	*tángcù lǐyú* 糖醋鲤鱼 *(tahng-tsu lee-yuu)*
mapo tofu	*mápó dòufu (mah-pwaw doe-foo)* 麻婆豆腐
Kung Pao chicken	*Gōng bǎo jī dīng (Gohng-bow jee-deeng)* 宫保鸡丁
fish flavored pork slices	*yúxiāng ròusī (yuu-shee-ahng roe-suh)* 鱼香肉丝
saliva chicken (chilled chicken in spicy bean paste)	*kǒushuǐ jī (koe-shway jee)* 口水鸡
dandan noodles	*dàndàn miàn (dahn-dahn mee-an)* 担担面
poached sliced fish in hot chili oil	*shuǐzhǔ yú (shway-joo yuu)* 水煮鱼
hotpot	*huǒguō (hwoh-gwoh)* 火锅
kelp / seaweed	*hǎidài (hi-die)* 海带
abalone	*bàoyú (bow-yuu)* 鲍鱼
sharkfin	*yúchì (yuu-chee)* 鱼翅
scallops	*gānbèi (gahn-bay)* 干贝
lobster	*lóngxiā (lohng-she-ah)* 龙虾

bird's nest	*yànwō (yahn-woh)* 燕窝
roast suckling pig	*kǎorǔ zhū (kow roo-joo)* 烤乳猪
preserved meat	*làròu (lah-roe)* 腊肉
barbecued pork	*chāshāo (chah-shou)* 叉烧
sausage	*xiāngcháng (shee-ahng chahng)* 香肠
fried pork flakes	*ròusōng (roo-sohng)* 肉松
local dish	*dìfang cài (dee-fahng tsigh)* 地方菜
set meal	*tàocān (tao-tsahn)* 套餐
fried rice	*chǎofàn (chaow-fahn)* 炒饭
plain rice	*báifàn (bye-fahn)* 白饭
crispy rice	*guōbā (gwo-bah)* 锅巴
porridge	*zhōu (joe)* 粥
noodles	*miàn (mee-an)* 面
clay pot	*shāguō (shah-gwoh)* 砂锅
meat bun	*ròu bāozi (roo bow-dzu)* 肉包子
preserved bean curd	*fǔrǔ (foo-roo)* 腐乳
fermented black bean	*dòuchǐ (doe-chee)* 豆豉
preserved egg	*pídàn (pee-dahn)* 皮蛋
salted duck egg	*xiányā dàn (shee-an yah-dahn)* 咸鸭蛋
crab meat	*xièròu (she-eh roo)* 蟹肉
prawn	*míng xiā (meeng-she-ah)* 明虾

I want to eat ____.
Wǒ yào chī ____. (Woh yow chee ____)
我要吃____。

Pay *Fùqián* *(Foo-chee-an)* 付钱

bill / check	*zhàngdān* *(jahng-dahn)* 帐单
credit card	*xìnyòngkǎ* *(sheen-yohng-kah)* 信用卡
traveler's checks	*lǚyóu zhīpiào* *(lwee-you jr-pee-ow)* 旅游支票

I want to pay the bill.
Wǒ yào fù zhàng.
(Woh yee-ow foo jahng) 我要付帐。

The bill, please.
Qǐng suàn zhàng. *(Cheeng swahn jahng)* 请算帐。

Separate checks, please.
Qǐng fēnkāi suàn.
(Cheeng fern-kigh swahn) 请分开算。

Do you take credit cards?
Nǐmen shōu xìnyòngkǎ ma? 你们收信用卡吗?
(Nee-mern show sheen-yohng kah mah)

Do you take traveler's checks?
Nǐmen shōu lǚyóu zhīpiào ma? 你们收旅游支票吗?
(Nee-mern show lwee-you jr-pee-ow mah)

A receipt, please.
Qǐng gěi shōujù.
(Cheeng gay show-jwee) 请给收据。

Do you have any / it / some?
Nǐ yǒu ma? (Nee you mah) 你有吗?

I have it / some.
Yǒu. (You) 有。

I don't have any / it.
Wǒ méiyǒu. (Woh may you) 我没有。

Do you have the tickets?
Nǐ yǒu piào ma? (Nee you pee-ow mah)
你有票吗?

Do you have _____?
Nǐ yǒu _____? (Nee you _____)
你有 _____?

boiled eggs	*zhǔ jīdàn (joo jee-dahn)* 煮鸡蛋	
boiled water	*kāishuǐ (kigh-shway)* 开水	
bottle opener	*kāipíngqì (kigh ping chee)* 开瓶器	
a boyfriend	*nánpéngyou (nahn perng-you)* 男朋友	
a calendar	*rìlì (ree-lee)* 日历	
a camera	*zhàoxiàngjī (Jow-she-ahng-jee)* 照相机	
dim sum	*diǎnxin (dee-an sheen)* 点心	
an envelope	*xìnfēng (sheen-ferng)* 信封	
a headache	*tóuténg (toe-terng)* 头疼	

Don't Have *Méiyǒu* (May You) 没有

I don't have my passport.
Wǒ méiyǒu hùzhào.
(Woh may you hoo-jow) 我没有护照。

I don't have any money.
Wǒ méiyǒu qián. (Woh may you chee-an) 我没有钱。

We don't have time.
Wǒmen méiyǒu shíjiān.
(Woh-mern may you shr-jee-an) 我们没有时间。

I don't have an umbrella.
Wǒ méiyǒu yǔsǎn.
(Woh may you yuh-sahn) 我没有雨伞。

I don't have a pen (ball point).
Wǒ méiyǒu yuánzhūbǐ. (Woh may you ywahn-joo-bee)
我没有圆珠笔。

Telephone *Diànhuà* (Dee-an-hwah) 电话

local call	*běndì diànhuà* *(bern-dee dee-an-hwah)* 本地电话
long-distance call	*chángtú diànhuà* *(chahng-too dee-an-hwah)* 长途电话
international call	*guójì diànhuà* *(gwoh-jee dee-an-hwah)* 国际电话
public telephone	*gōngyòng diànhuà* 公用电话 *(gohng-yohng dee-an-hwah)*

I want to make a phone call.
Wǒ xiǎng dǎ diànhuà.
(Woh she-ahng dah dee-an-hwah) 我想打电话。

I want to make an international call.
Wǒ yào dǎ yīgè guójì chángtú diànhuà.
(Woh yee-ow dah ee-guh gwoh-jee chahng-too dee-an-hwah) 我要打一个国际长途电话。

I want to call long-distance.
Wǒ xiǎng dǎ chángtú.
(Woh she-ahng dah chahng-too) 我想打长途。

May I use your phone?
Wǒ kěyǐ yòng nǐ de diànhuà ma?
(Woh ker-ee yohng nee der dee-an-hwah mah)
我可以用你的电话吗?

A collect call, please.
Duìfāng fùkuǎn.
(Dway-fahng foo-kwahn) 对方付款。

What is your telephone number?
Nǐ de diànhuà hàomǎ shì?
(Nee-der dee-an-hwah how-mah shr) 你的电话号码是?

My telephone number is _____.
Wǒ de diànhuà hàomǎ shì _____.
(Woh der dee-an-hwah how-mah shr _____)
我的电话号码是 _____。

I want to send a fax.
Xiǎng dǎ chuánzhēn.
(She-ahng dah chwan zhern) 想打传真。

Cell Phone *Shǒujī* *(show jee)* 手机

Do you have a cell phone?
Yǒu shǒujī ma? *(You show jee mah?)* 有手机吗?

I want to buy / rent a cell phone.
Wǒ yào mǎi / zū shǒujī.
(Woh yee-ow my / joo show jee) 我要 买／租 手机。

Where can I buy a cell phone? 哪里可以买手机?
Nǎlǐ kěyǐ mǎi shǒujī? *(Nah-lee kuh-ee my show jee)*

Let's take a selfie!
Wǒmen zì pāi ba!
(Wor-mern her-jow bah) 我们自拍吧!

My phone is out of battery!
Wǒ de shǒujī méi diàn le!
(Woh der show-jee may-dee-an ler) 我的手机没电了!

Do you have a Charge-pal (back-up battery for cell phones)?
Nǐ yǒu chōng diàn bǎo ma?
(Nee you chohng dee-an bow mah?) 你有充电宝吗?

I need to recharge ....
Wǒ xūyào gěi .... chōng diàn. 我需要给…充电。
(Woh shee-yee-ow gay ... chohng-dee-an)

Do you have Blue-tooth?
Nǐ yǒu lányá ma?
(Nee you lahn-yah mah) 你有蓝牙吗?

Do you have GPS?
Nǐ yǒu GPS ma? (Nee you GPS mah)
你有GPS吗?

Bad reception! (phone)
Xìnhào bùhǎo! (Sheen-how boo-how) 信号不好!

Is there Internet connection here?
Zhèlǐ néng shàngwǎng ma?
(Juh-lee nerng shahng-wahng mah) 这里能上网吗?

Is there mobile-Internet connection here?
Zhèlǐ néng yídòng shàngwǎng ma?
(Juh-lee nerng ee-doong shahng-wahng mah)
这里能移动上网吗?

Is there Wi-Fi connection here?
Zhèlǐ yǒu Wi-Fi ma?
(Juh-lee you Wifi mah) 这里有 Wi-Fi 吗?

What's the Wi-Fi password?
Wi-Fi mìmǎ shì duōshao?
(Wifi me-mah shr dwoh-shou) Wi-Fi 密码是多少?

I have an Android phone.
Wǒ yǒu ānzhuó shǒujī.
(Woh you ahn-jwoh show-jee) 我有安卓手机。

I have an iPhone.
Wǒ yǒu iPhone. (Woh you iPhone) 我有iPhone。

I don't have a smartphone.
Wǒ méiyǒu zhìnéng shǒujī.
(Woh may-you jr-nerng show-jee) 我没有智能手机。

Do you want to voice-chat?
Nǐ xiǎng yǔyīn liáotiān ma? 你想语音聊天吗?
(Nee shee-ahng yuu-een lee-ow-tee-an mah)

Do you want to video-chat?
Nǐ xiǎng shìpín liáotiān ma? 你想视频聊天吗?
(Nee shee-ahng shr-peen lee-ow-tee-an mah)

Let's chat online!
Wǒmen wǎngshàng liáo ba! 我们网上聊吧!
(Woh-mern wahng-shahng lee-ow bah)

Computer *Diànnǎo* (Dee-an-now) 电脑 / *Jìsuànjī* (Jee-swahn-jee) 计算机

61

computer hardware	*yìngjiàn* (eeng-jee-an) 硬件
computer software	*ruǎnjiàn* (roo-an-jee-an) 软件
cord	*diànxiàn* (dee-an-she-an) 电线
modem	*tiáozhì jiětiáoqì* 调制解调器 (tee-ow jr jay tee-ow chee)
hard disk	*yìngpán* (eeng-pahn) 硬盘
CD disk	*CD guāngdié* (Cee-Dee guang-deen) CD光碟
computer mouse	*diànnǎo shǔbiāo* (dee-an-now shuu-biao) 电脑鼠标
printer	*dǎyìnjī* (dah-een jee) 打印机
English word processing	*Yīngwén wénzì chǔlǐ* (Eeng-wern wern-dzu choo-lee) 英文文字处理

I don't have a computer.
Wǒ méiyǒu jìsuànjī / diànnǎo.
(Woh may you jee-swahn-jee/dee-an-now)
我没有 计算机 / 电脑。

May I use a computer?
Wǒ kěyǐ yòng diànnǎo ma?
(Woh-ker-ee yohng dee-an-now mah) 我可以用电脑吗?

I want to buy a disk holder.
Wǒ xiǎng mǎi cípán jià.
(Woh she-ahng my tsu-pahn jah) 我想买磁盘架。

Internet / E-mail *Yīngtèwǎng (Eeng-ter-wahng)* 英特网 / *Diànzǐ yóujiàn (Dee-an-dzu you jee-an)* 电子邮件

I would like to check my email.
Wǒ xiǎng chá wǒ de diànzǐ yóujiàn.
(Woh she-ahng chah woh-der dee-an-dzu you-jee-an)
我想查我的电子邮件。

Where can I go to get on the Internet?
Dào nǎlǐ qù shàng Yīngtèwǎng?
(Dow nah-lee chwee shahng Eeng-ter-wahng)
到哪里去上英特网?

Is there an Internet café?
Yǒu wǎngbā ma? (You wang-baah mah) 有网吧吗?

I want to search the Internet.
Wǒ xiǎng chá Yīngtèwǎng.
(Woh she-ahng cha Eeng-ter-wahng) 我想查英特网。

How much is it per hour?
Yī gè xiǎoshí duōshao qián?
(Ee-guh she-ow-shr dwoh-shou chee-an)
一个小时多少钱?

What is your email address?
Nǐ de diànzǐ yóujiàn xìnxiāng shì shénme? *(Nee-der
dee-an-dzu you jee-an sheen-she-ahng shr-shern-mo)*
你的电子邮件信箱是什么?

Because of the policy set by the Chinese government,
Facebook, Twitter, Google, Instagram, etc. are still banned
in mainland China. As a result, Chinese local service
providers flourish.

Do you have Twitter?
Nǐ yǒu Tuītè ma? (Nee you Twitter / tway-ter mah)
你有 Twitter／推特 吗?

Do you have Facebook?
Nǐ yǒu Facebook / liǎnshū ma?
(Nee you Facebook / lee-an-shoo mah)
你有 Facebook／脸书 吗?

What's your (Facebook, Twitter, Instagram, etc) ID?
Nǐ de … yònghùmíng shì shénme?
(Nee der … yohng-hoo-meeng shr shern-mer)
你的…用户名是什么?

Do you have QQ?
Nǐ yǒu QQ ma? (Nee you QQ mah) 你有QQ吗?

What's your QQ number?
Nǐ de QQ hàomǎ shì duōshao? 你的QQ号码是多少?
(Nee der QQ how-mah shr dwoh-shou)

My QQ number is....
Wǒde QQ hàomǎ shì…
(woh der QQ how-mah shr...) 我的QQ号码是…

Do you have Wei Xin (Wechat)?
Nǐ yǒu Wēixìn ma?
(Nee you way-sheen mah) 你有微信吗?

What's your Wei Xin ID?
Nǐ de Wēixìn yònghùmíng / ID shì shénme?
(nee der way-sheen yohng-hoo-meeng shr shern-mer)
你的微信用户名／ID是什么?

My Wei Xin number/ID is....
Wǒde Wēixìn yònghùmíng / ID shì ….
(Woh der way-sheen yohng-hoo-meeng shr...)
我的微信用户名／ID是…

Do you have Weibo?
Nǐ yǒu Wēibó ma?
(Nee you way-bwo mah) 你有微博吗?

What's your Weibo ID?
Nǐ de Wēibó yònghùmíng shì shénme?
(Nee der way-bwo yohng-hoo-meeng shr shern-mer)
你的微博用户名是什么?

Do you play video games?
Nǐ wán shìpín yóuxì ma?
(Nee wahn shee-ping you-she mah) 你玩视频游戏吗?

Do you play online games?
Nǐ wán wǎngluò yóuxì ma? 你玩网络游戏吗?
(nee wahn wahng-lwaw you-she mah)

I'm online.
Wǒ zàixiàn. (Woh zigh-shee-an) 我在线。

I'm offline.
Wǒ búzài xiàn.
(Woh boo zigh-shee-an) 我不在线 。

Are you online / offline?
Nǐ zàixiàn / bùzài xiàn ma? 你 在线 ／ 不在线 吗？
(Nee zigh-shee-an / boo-zigh-sheen-an mah)

63 Seasons *Jìjié* *(Jee-jeh)* 季节

spring	*chūnjì (chwun-jee)* 春季	
springtime	*zài chūntiān*	
	(zigh chwun-tee-an) 在春天	
summer	*xiàjì (shee-ah-jee)* 夏季	
summertime	*zài xiàtiān*	
	(zigh shee-ah-tee-an) 在夏天	
fall	*qiūjì (chew-jee)* 秋季	
autumn	*qiūtiān (chew-tee-an)* 秋天	
winter	*dōngjì (dohng-jee)* 冬季	

What is the best season in Beijing?
Běijīng de nǎ yī ge jìjié zuìhǎo?
(Bay-jeeng-der nah-ee guh jee-jeh zway-how)
北京的哪一个季节最好？

When does spring begin?
Chūntiān shénme shíhou kāishǐ?
(Chwun-tee-an shern-mo shr-hoe kigh-shr)
春天什么时候开始？

Is it hot during the summer?
Xiàtiān rè ma? (Shee-ah tee-an ruh mah) 夏天热吗?

What is the best season in Shanghai?
Shànghǎi de nǎ yī ge jìjié zuìhǎo?
(Shahng-high-der nah-ee guh jee-jeh zway-how)
上海的哪一个季节最好?

Does it get cold in Guangzhou in winter?
Guǎngzhōu dōngtiān lěng ma?
(Gwahng-joe doong-tee-an lerng mah) 广州冬天冷吗?

---

64   Weather *Tiānqì* *(Tee-an-chee)* 天气

temperature *wēndù* (wern-doo) 温度

weather forecast   *tiānqì yùbào*
(tee-an-chee yuu-bow) 天气预报

How is the weather today?
Jīntiān tiānqì zěnmeyàng?
(Jeen-tee-an tee-an-chee zen-mo-yahng)
今天天气怎么样?

What is the temperature?
Wēndù yǒu duōshao?
(Wern-doo you dwoh show) 温度有多少?

It's cold!
Mán lěng de! (Mahn lerng der) 蛮冷的!

It's hot!
Mán rè de! (Mahn ruh der) 蛮热的!

It's sunny.
Yǒu tàiyang. (You tie-yahng) 有太阳。

It's bad.
Bùhǎo. (Boo how) 不好。

It's windy.
Yǒufēng. (You ferng) 有风。

It's windy!
Fēng dà! (Ferng dah) 风大！

It's raining.
Xiàyǔ le. (Shee-ah yuu ler) 下雨了。

It's snowing.
Xiàxuě le. (Shee-ah she-eh luh) 下雪了。

Meet / Meeting *Jiàn* (Jee-an) 见 / *Huì* (Hway) 会

65

Please meet me at my hotel.
Qǐng zài wǒ de lǚguǎn jiàn.
(Cheeng dzigh woh-der lwee-gwahn jee-an)
请在我的旅馆见。

What time shall I come?
Wǒ shénme shíhou lái?
(Woh shern-mo shr hoe lie) 我什么时候来？

I'm sorry I'm late.
Hěn bàoqiàn lái wǎn le.
(Hern bow-chee-an lie-wahn-ler) 很抱歉来晚了。

What time does the meeting start?
Huìyì jǐdiǎn kāishǐ?
(Hway-ee jee-dee-an kigh shr?) 会议几点开始?

66 Buy *Mǎi* (My) 买

I want to buy _____.
Wǒ xiǎng mǎi _____. (Woh she-ahng my _____)
我想买 _____。

antiques	*gǔdǒng (goo-dohng)* 古董	
apples	*píngguǒ (peeng-gwoh)* 苹果	
bananas	*xiāngjiāo (shee-ahng-jow)* 香蕉	
books	*shū (shoo)* 书	
cashew nuts	*yāoguǒ (yow-gwoh)* 腰果	
flashlight	*shǒudiàntǒng (show-dee-an-tohng)* 手电筒	
jacket	*jiākè (jah-ker)* 夹克	
lacquerware	*qīqì (chee-chee)* 漆器	
mineral water	*kuàngquán shuǐ (kwahng-chwahn shway)* 矿泉水	
posters	*zhāotiēhuà (jow-tee-eh-hwah)* 招贴画	
tea set	*chájù (chah-jwee)* 茶具	

I would like an English-Chinese dictionary.
Wǒ xiǎng yào yīběn Yīng Hànzì zìdiǎn.
(Woh she-ahng yow ee-bern Eeng-Hahn dzu-dee-an)
我想要一本英汉字典。

I want to buy a tourist map.
Wǒ yào mǎi yīzhāng lǚyóu tú. 我要买一张旅游图。
(Woh yow my ee jahng lwee-you too)

98

Shopping *Mǎi dōngxi* *(My-dohng-she)* 买东西

shopping center	*shāngchǎng* *(shahng-chahng)* 商场
shop / store	*shāngdiàn* *(shahng-dee-an)* 商店
department store	*bǎihuò gōngsī* *(by-hwoh gohng-sr)* 百货公司
street market	*shìchǎng* *(she-chahng)* 市场
bookstore	*shūdiàn* *(shoo-dee-an)* 书店

Where can I buy an umbrella?
Nǎlǐ kěyǐ mǎi yǔsǎn?
(Nah-lee ker-ee my yuu-sahn) 哪里可以买雨伞?

Is there a department store near here?
Zhè fùjìn yǒu bǎihuò gōngsī ma?
(Jur foo-jeen yoh by-hwoh gohng-sr mah)
这附近有百货公司吗?

What time do you open?
Nǐmen shénme shíhou kāimén?
(Nee-mern shern-mo shr-hoe kigh-mern)
你们什么时候开门?

I want to go to a street market.
Wǒ yào qù shìchǎng.
(Woh yee-ow chwee shr-chahng) 我要去市场。

How much is this in US dollars?
Zhè zhí duōshao Měiyuán?
(Jur jr dwoh-show May ywahn) 这值多少美元?

I'm just looking.
Wǒ suíbiàn kànkan. *(Woh shway-ban kahn-kahn)*
我随便看看。

I'd like a raincoat, please.
Qǐng gěi wǒ yǔyī. (Cheeng gay woh yuu-ee)
请给我雨衣。

I'd like a pair of sandals, please.
Wǒ xiǎng mǎi liǎngxié.
(Wo she-ahng my lee-ahng-shay) 我想买凉鞋。

I need some razor blades.
Wǒ xūyào guāhú dāo.
(Woh shee yee-ow gwah-hoo dow) 我需要刮胡刀。

I need some sanitary napkins.
Wǒ xūyào wèishēng jǐn.
(Woh shee yee-ow (way sherng jeen) 我需要卫生巾。

I need some toilet paper.
Wǒ xūyào wèishēngzhǐ.
(Woh shee yee-ow way-sherng jr) 我需要卫生纸。

I am looking for _____.
Wǒ zài zhǎo _____. (Woh zigh jow _____)
我在找 _____。

How much is this?
Zhè ge duōshao qián?
(Jay-guh dwoh shou chee-an) 这个多少钱?

How much is that?
Nà ge duōshao qián?
(Nah-guh dwoh-shou chee-an) 那个多少钱?

I want that.
Wǒ yào nà ge. (Woh yee-ow nah-guh) 我要那个。

May I have a receipt?
Néng gěi wǒ yīgè shōujù ma? 能给我一个收据吗?
(Nerng gay woh ee-guh show jwee mah)

Do you take US dollars?
Nǐmen shōu Měiyuán ma?
(Nee-mern show May ywahn mah) 你们收美元吗?

Do you take British pounds?
Nǐmen shōu Yīngbàng ma?
(Nee-mern show Eeng bahng mah) 你们收英磅吗?

Do you take traveler's checks?
Nǐmen shōu lǚyóu zhīpiào ma? 你们收旅游支票吗?
(Nee-mern show lwee-you jr-pee-ow mah)

Do you take credit cards?
Nǐmen shōu xìnyòngkǎ ma? 你们收信用卡吗?
(Nee-mern show sheeng-yohng kah mah)

68 Gifts *Lǐwù* (Lee-woo) 礼物

gift shop	*lǐpǐn diàn* (lee-peen dee-an) 礼品店	
antique shop	*gǔdǒng diàn* (goo-dohng dee-an) 古董店	
jewelry store	*zhūbǎo diàn* (joo-bow dee-an) 珠宝店	
bookstore	*shūdiàn* (shoo-dee-an) 书店	

Please show me _____.
Qǐng gěi wǒ kàn _____.
(Cheeng gay woh kahn _____) 请给我看 _____。

I want to buy _____.
Wǒ yào mǎi _____.
(Woh yee-ow my _____) 我要买 _____。

May I see that?
Wǒ kěyǐ kàn nà ge ma?
(Woh ker-ee-kahn na-guh mah) 我可以看那个吗?

May I look at it?
Wǒ néng kàn ma?
(Woh nerng kahn mah) 我能看吗?

69 Cost / Price *Jiàgé* *(Jah-guh)* 价格

Can you tell me the price?
Nǐmen néng bào yīxià jiàgé ma?
(Nee mern nerng bow ee-shee-ah jah-guh mah)
你们能报一下价格吗?

How much is this?
Zhè ge duōshao? *(Jay-guh dwoh-shou)* 这个多少?

Is the price negotiable?
Kěyǐ jiǎng jià ma?
(Ker-ee jee-ahng jah mah) 可以讲价吗?

That one is too expensive.
Nà yī gè tài guì.
(Nah ee-guh tie gway) 那一个太贵。

Newsstand *Bàotíng* (Bow-teeng) 报亭 / *Bàotān* (Bow-tahn) 报摊

Do you have (is there) a newsstand?
Yŏu bàotān ma? (You bow-tahn mah) 有报摊吗?

Where is it?
Tā zài nălĭ? (Tah zigh nah-lee) 它在哪里?

Do you have English language newspapers?
Yŏu Yīngwén bàozhĭ ma?
(You Eeng-wern bow-jr mah) 有英文报纸吗?

I'd like to buy this magazine.
Zhè zázhì wŏ yào măi.
(Jur zah-jr woh yee-ow my) 这杂志我要买。

I want to buy this book.
Zhè bĕn shū wŏ yào măi.
(Jur-ben shoo woh yee-ow my) 这本书我要买。

Post Office *Yóujú* (You Jwee) 邮局

mail	*xìn (sheen)* 信
mail (verb)	*jì xìn (jee sheen)* 寄信
mailbox	*yóutŏng (you-tohng)* 邮筒
airmail	*háng yóu (hahng-you)* 航邮
postage stamp	*yóupiào (you pee-ow)* 邮票

Where is the nearest post office?
Zuìjìn de yóujú zài nălĭ? 最近的邮局在哪里?
(Zway-jeen-der you jwee zigh nah-lee)

How do I get to the post office?
Dào yóujú zěnme zǒu?
(Dow you-jwee zern mo dzow) 到邮局怎么走?

Please mail this.
Qǐng jì zhè jiàn. (Cheeng jee jur jee-an) 请寄这件。

72 Sightseeing *Guānguāng* (Gwahn-gwahng) 观光

I want to go sightseeing.
Wǒ yào qù guānguāng.
(Woh yee-ow chwee gwahn-gwahng) 我要去观光。

I want to go to the Great Wall.
Wǒ yào qù Chángchéng.
(Woh yee-ow chwee Chahng Cherng) 我要去长城。

How far is it?
Lí zhè duō yuǎn? (Lee jur dwoh ywahn) 离这多远?

How long will it take?
Zhè yào duō cháng de shíjiān? 这要多长的时间?
(Jur yee-ow dwoh chahng der shr-jee-an?)

Where is _____?
_____ *zài nǎ?* (_____ zigh nah-urr)
_____ 在哪?

Can I walk there?
Wǒ kěyǐ zǒu lù ma?
(Woh ker-ee dzow loo mah) 我可以走路吗?

May we come in?
Kěyǐ jìnlái ma? (Ker-ee jeen-lie mah) 可以进来吗?

May I / we wait here?
Zhè kěyǐ děng ma?
(Jur ker-ee derng mah) 这可以等吗?

May I / we take photos here?
Zhè kěyǐ zhàoxiàng ma?
(Jur ker-ee jow-she-ahng mah) 这可以照相吗?

73 See *kàn* (kahn) 看

We want to see the Great Wall.
Wǒmen xiǎng kàn Chángchéng. 我们想看长城。
(Woh-mern shee-ahng kahn Chahng Cherng)

Have you seen the Great Wall?
Nǐ kàn guò Chángchéng ma?
(Nee kahn gwoh Chahng Cherng) 你看过长城吗?

We want to see Tianamen Square.
Wǒmen xiǎng kàn Tiānānmén. 我们想看天安门。
(Woh-mern shee-ahng kahn Tee-an-ahn-mern)

74 Travel Agent *Lǚxíngshè* (Lwee-sheeng Sher) 旅行社

We would like to see the downtown area.
Wǒmen xiǎng qù kàn shì zhōngxīn.
(Woh-mern she-ahng chwee kahn shr johng-sheen)
我们想去看市中心。

Can you arrange a tour of the area?
Nǐ néng ānpái běndì yóu ma? 你能安排本地游吗?
(Nee nerng ahn-pie bern-dee you mah)

How long is the tour?
Lǚyóu yào duō jiǔ?
(Lwee you yee-ow dwoh jew) 旅游要多久?

Is it all right to take photographs?
Kěyǐ zhàoxiàng ma?
(Ker-ee jow-she-ahng mah) 可以照相吗?

75 **Martial Arts** *Wǔshù* (Woo-shoo) 武术

I'd like to see a martial arts exhibition.
Wǒ xiǎng kàn wǔshù biǎoyǎn. 我想看武术表演。
(Woh she-ahng kahn woo-shoo bee-ow-yahn)

Where can I see a martial arts exhibition?
Wǔshù biǎoyǎn zài nǎlǐ? 武术表演在哪里?
(Woo-shoo bee-ow-yahn zigh nah-lee)

Is there a fee?
Yào shōufèi ma? *(yee-ow show fay mah)* 要收费吗?

How much is it?
Duōshao qián? *(Dwoh-shou chee-an)* 多少钱?

76 **Peking (Beijing) Opera** *Jīngjù* (Jeeng Jwee)
京剧

I want to go to the Beijing Opera.
Wǒ yào qù kàn Jīngjù.
(Woh yee-ow chwee kahn Jeeng Jwee) 我要去看京剧。

What is on tonight?
Jīntiān wǎnshang shénme jiémù? *(Jee-an-tee-an wahn-shang shern-mo jeh-moo)* 今天晚上什么节目?

What is the name / title (of the play)?
(Biǎoyǎn) Jiào shénme míngzi?
([Bee-ow-yahn] Jow shern-mo meeng-dzu)
(表演) 叫什么名字?

What time will it begin?
Shénme shíhou kāishǐ?
(Shern-mo shr-hoe kigh-shr)
什么时候开始?

Are the performers famous?
Yǎnyuán chūmíng ma?
(Yahn-ywahn choo-meeng mah) 演员出名吗?

How long will it last?
Yǎn duō cháng shíjiān?
(Yahn dwoh-chahng shr-jee-an) 演多长时间?

Where can I buy tickets?
Zài nǎli kěyǐ mǎi dào piào? 在哪里可以买到票?
(Dzigh nah-lee ker-ee my-dow pee-ow)

Is it necessary to buy tickets in advance?
Yīdìng yào tíqián mǎi piào ma?
(Ee-deeng yee-ow tee-chee-an my pee-ow mah)
一定要提前买票吗?

Emergency *Jǐnjí qíngkuàng* *(Jeen-jee cheeng-kwahng)*紧急情况

I've lost my camera.
Wǒ diū le zhàoxiàngjǐ.
(Woh dew-ler jow-she-ahng-jee) 我丢了照相机。

Someone has stolen my money.
Yǒurén tōu le wǒ de qián. 有人偷了我的钱。
(you-wren tow-ler woh der chee-an)

Someone has stolen my passport.
Yǒurén tōu le wǒ de hùzhào. 有人偷了我的护照。
(you-wren tow-ler woh der hoo-jow)

Someone has stolen my purse.
Yǒurén tōu le wǒ de qiánbāo. 有人偷了我的钱包。
(you-wren tow-ler woh der chee-an-bow)

Help! (shout)
Jiùmìng ā! *(Jew-meeng-ah)* 救命啊!

78 III / Sick *Bìng* *(Beeng)* 病

I'm sick.
Wǒ bìng le. *(Woh beeng ler)*. 我病了。

I don't feel well.
Wǒ gǎnjué bùhǎo.
(Woh gahn-jway boo how) 我感觉不好。

It is very serious.
Hěn yánzhòng. *(Hern yahn-johng)* 很严重。

I have a pain in my chest.
Wǒ xiōng téng. *(Woh shee-ong terng)* 我胸疼。

I have a pain in my stomach.
Wǒ wèi téng. *(Woh way terng)* 我胃疼。

I feel dizzy.
Wǒ juéde tóuyūn.
(Woh jway-der toe ywun) 我觉得头晕。

I have a fever.
Wǒ fāshāo le. (Woh fah-shou-ler) 我发烧了。

I have a heart condition.
Wǒ yǒu xīnzàngbìng.
(Woh you sheen-dzahng beeng) 我有心脏病。

I have diabetes.
Wǒ yǒu tángniàobìng.
(Woh you tahng-nee-ow beeng) 我有糖尿病。

I have a headache.
Wǒ yǒu diǎn tóu tòng.
(Woh you dee-an toe-tohng) 我有点头痛。

---

79 **Medicine** *Yīyào (Ee-yee-ow)* 医药 ·

drugstore (pharmacy)	*yàofáng (yee-ow-fahng)* 药房
aspirin	*āsīpǐlín (ah-srn-pee-leen)* 阿司匹林
eye drops	*yǎn yàoshuǐ (yahn yee-ow shway)* 眼药水
cough medicine	*késou yào (ker-soh yee-ow)* 咳嗽药

Where is a pharmacy?
Yàofáng zài nǎlǐ?
(Yee-ow-fahng dzigh nah-lee) 药房在哪里?

What time does the pharmacy open?
Yàofáng jǐdiǎn kāi?
(Yee-ow-fahng jee-dee-an kigh) 药房几点开?

I'd like some aspirin.
Wǒ xiǎng yào āsīpǐlín. 我想要阿司匹林。
(Woh she-ahng yee-ow ah-sr-pee-leen)

I'd like some eye drops.
Wǒ xiǎng yào yǎn yàoshuǐ. 我想要眼药水。
(Woh she-ahng yee-ow yahn yee-ow shway)

I'd like something for a cold.
Wǒ xiǎng mǎi gǎnmào yào. 我想买感冒药。
(Woh she-ahng-my gahn mao yee-ow)

I'd like something for a cough.
Wǒ xiǎng mǎi késou yào.
(Woh she-ahng-my ker-soh yee-ow) 我想买咳嗽药。

I'd like some contraceptives.
Wǒ xiǎng yào bìyùn yào. 我想要避孕药。
(Woh she-ahng yee-ow bee-ywun yee-ow)

80

Doctor *Yīshēng* *(Ee-sherng)* 医生 / *Dàifu*
(Die-foo) 大夫

I need to see a doctor.
Wǒ yào kàn yīshēng.
(Woh yee-ow kahn ee-sherng) 我要看医生。

Is there a doctor who speaks English?
Yǒu néng shuō Yīngwén de yīshēng ma?
(You nerng shwo Eeng wern der ee-sherng mah)
有能说英文的医生吗?

Please call a doctor for me.
Qǐng gěi wǒ jiào yīshēng.
(Cheeng gay woh jow ee-sherng) 请给我叫医生。

Call a doctor quickly!
Gǎnkuài jiào yīshēng!
(Gahn-kwie jow ee-sherng) 赶快叫医生!

Please prescribe Western medicine.
Qǐng gěi wǒ Xīyào.
(Cheeng gay woh She-yee-ow) 请给我西药。

81 Dentist *Yáyī* *(yah-ee)* 牙医

I have a toothache.
Wǒ yá téng. (Woh yah terng) 我牙疼。

I've broken a tooth.
Wǒ de yáchǐ duàn le.
(Woh der yah-chr dwahn-ler) 我的牙齿断了。

I've lost a filling.
Wǒ de yá tiánliào diū le.
(Woh der yah tee-an lee-ow dew-ler) 我的牙填料丢了。

I need to go to a dentist.
Wǒ yào qù kàn yáyī.
(Woh yee-ow chwee kahn yah-ee) 我要去看牙医。

Can you recommend a dentist?
Nǐ jièshào yīgè yáyī hǎo ma? 你介绍一个牙医好吗?
(Nee jeh-shou ee-guh yah-ee how mah)

82 Hospital *Yīyuàn* *(Ee-ywahn)* 医院

Western hospital	*Xīyīyuàn (She-ee ywahn)* 西医院	
emergency room	*jízhěnshì (jee-zhern shr)* 急诊室	
accident	*shìgù (shr-goo)* 事故	

Is there a hospital near here?
Zhè fùjìn yǒu yīyuàn ma?
(Jur foo-jeen you ee-ywahn mah) 这附近有医院吗?

Take me to a hospital.
Sòng wǒ dào yīyuàn qù.
(Sohng woh dow ee-ywahn chwee) 送我到医院去。

I want to go to a Western hospital.
Wǒ yào qù Xīyīyuàn.
(Woh yee-ow chwee she-ee ywahn) 我要去西医院。

83 Ambulance *Jiùhùchē* *(Jew-hoo-cher)* 救护车

Please call an ambulance!
Qǐng kuài jiào jiùhùchē!
(Cheeng kwai jee-ow jew-hoo-cher) 请快叫救护车!

It's urgent!
Hěn jí! (Hern jee) 很急!

Take me (him / her) to the hospital!
Sòng wǒ (tā) dào yīyuàn qù! (Sohng woh (tah) dow
ee-ywahn chwee) 送我 (他／她) 到医院去!

She was hit by a car!
Tā bèi qìchē zhuàngdào le! (Tah bay chee-cher joo-
ahng dow-ler) 她被汽车撞到了!

84 Police *Jǐngchá* (Jeeng-chah) 警察

"People's police" *Rénmín jǐngchá* 人民警察
(Wren-meen jeeng-chah)

police station *jǐngchájú*
(jeeng-chah jwee) 警察局

Call the police!
Kuài jiào jǐngchá!
(Kwai jee-ow jeeng-chah) 快叫警察!

Someone has stolen my money.
Yǒurén tōu le wǒ de qián. 有人偷了我的钱。
(you-wren tow-ler woh-der chee-an)

Someone has stolen my watch.
Yǒurén tōu le wǒ de shǒubiǎo. 有人偷了我的手表。
(you-wren tow-ler woh-der show-bee-ow)

Embassy *Dàshǐguǎn* *(Dah-shr-gwahn)* 大使馆

I want to go to the American embassy.
Wǒ yào qù Měiguó dàshǐguǎn. 我要去美国大使馆。
(Woh yee-ow chwee May-gwoh dah-shr-gwahn)

I want to go to the ____.
Wǒ yào qù ____. *(Woh yee-ow chwee ____)* 我要去____。

Australian embassy	*Aodàliyà dàshǐguǎn* *(Ow-dah-lee-yah dah-shr-gwahn)* 澳大利亚大使馆
Belgian embassy	*Bǐlìshí dàshǐguǎn* *(Bee-lee-shr...)* 比利时大使馆
British embassy	*Yīngguó dàshǐguǎn* *(Eeng-gwoh...)* 英国大使馆
Canadian embassy	*Jiānádà dàshǐguǎn* *(Jah-nah-dah ...)* 加拿大大使馆
French embassy	*Fǎguó dàshǐguǎn* *(Fah-gwoh ...)* 法国大使馆
German embassy	*Déguó dàshǐguǎn* *(Der-gwoh ...)* 德国大使馆
Italian embassy	*Yìdàlì dàshǐguǎn* *(Ee-dah-lee ...)* 意大利大使馆
New Zealand embassy	*Niǔxīlán dàshǐguǎn* *(New-she-lahn...)* 纽西兰大使馆
Portuguese embassy	*Pútáoyá dàshǐguǎn* *(Poo-tou-yah...)* 葡萄牙大使馆
Spanish embassy	*Xībānyá dàshǐguǎn* *(She-bahn-yah...)* 西班牙大使馆

86 **Lost** *Diū le* (dew-ler) 丢了

lose (the way)	*mí lù* (mee-loo) 迷路
lost (object)	*diū* (dew) 丢
Lost-and-Found	*Shìwù zhāolǐng chù* 事物招领处
	(Shr-woo Jow-leeng choo)

I'm lost.
Wǒ mí lù le. (Woh mee-loo-ler) 我迷路了。

I've lost my camera.
Wǒ diū le zhàoxiàngjī.
(Woh dew-ler jao shee-ahng jee) 我丢了照相机。

I've lost my luggage.
Wǒ diū le xíngli.
(Woh dew-ler sheeng-lee) 我丢了行李 。

87 **Barber Shop** *Lǐfà guǎn* (Lee-fah gwahn) 理发馆

haircut	*lǐfà* (lee-fah) 理发
shave	*guā liǎn* (gwah lee-an) 刮脸
beard	*húxū* (hoo-she) 胡须
massage	*ànmó* (ahn-moh) 按摩

I want a haircut.
Wǒ yào lǐfà.
(Woh yee-ow lee-fah) 我要理发。

I want a shave.
Wǒ yào guā liǎn.
(Woh yee-ow gwah lee-an) 我要刮脸。

Please trim my beard.
Qǐng xiū wǒ de húxū.
(Cheeng show woh-der hoo-she) 请修我的胡须。

Please massage my head.
Qǐng ànmó wǒ de tóubù. 请按摩我的头部。
(Cheeng ahn-moh woh-der toe-boo)

Beauty Parlor *Měiróng yuàn (May-rohng ywahn)* 美容院

facial massage	*miànbù ànmó* (mee-an-boo ahn-moh) 面部按摩
haircut	*lǐfà* (lee-fa) 理发
shampoo	*xǐ tóu* (she toe) 洗头
manicure	*xiū zhǐjia* (shew jr-jah) 修指甲
wash and blow dry	*xǐ hòu chuīgān* (she hoe chway-gahn) 洗后吹干

Is there a beauty parlor in the hotel?
Lǚguǎn yǒu měiróng yuàn ma? 旅馆有美容院吗?
(Lwee-gwahn you may rohng ywahn mah)

I'd like to make an appointment for tomorrow.
Wǒ xiǎng yùdìng zài míngtiān. 我想预定在明天。
(Woh she-ahng yuu-deeng dzigh meeng-tee-an)

Please give me a permanent.
Qǐng wèi wǒ tàng tóufa.
(Cheeng way woh tahng toe-fah) 请为我烫头发。

Please give me a shampoo.
Qǐng wèi wǒ xǐ tóu.
(Cheeng way woh she toe) 请为我洗头。

89 **Student** *Xuésheng* (Shway-sherng) 学生

I'm a student.
Wǒ shì xuésheng. (Woh shr shway-sherng) 我是学生。

Here is my student card.
Zhè shì wǒ de xuéshengzhèng. 这是我的学生证。
(Jur shr woh-der shway-sherng zherng)

Can you give me a discount?
Néng dǎ zhékòu ma?
(Nerng dah juh-koe mah) 能打折扣吗?

90 **Read** *kàn* (kahn) 看; *Dú* (Doo) 读

I cannot read Chinese.
Wǒ búhuì kàn Zhōngwén.
(Woh boo hway kahn Johng-wern) 我不会看中文。

Please read it to me.
Qǐng gěi wǒ dú zhège.
(Cheeng gay woh doo jur-guh) 请给我读这个。

Please read it out loud.
Qǐng dàshēng dú.
(Cheeng dah sherng doo) 请大声读。

Can you read English?
Nǐ néng dú Yīngwén ma?
(Nee nerng doo Eeng-wern) 你能读英文吗?

Can you read Romanized Chinese?
Nǐ néng dú Pīnyīn ma?
(Nee nerng doo Peen Een mah) 你能读拼音吗?

91 **Mistake** *Cuòwù* *(Tswoh-woo)* 错误 / *Cuòshì*
(Tswoh-shr) 错事

Excuse me, I think I made a mistake.
Duìbuqǐ, wǒ zuò le yī jiàn cuòshì.
(Dway-boo-chee, woh zwoh-ler ee-jee-an tswoh-shr)
对不起，我做了一件错事。

Excuse me, I think you made a mistake.
Duìbuqǐ, nǐ zuò le yī jiàn cuòshì.
(Dway-boo-chee nee zwoh-ler ee-jee-an tswoh-shr)
对不起，你做了一件错事。

He made a mistake.
Tā zuò le yī jiàn cuòshì.
(Tah zwoh-ler ee-jee-an tswoh-shr) 他做了一件错事。

That is not a mistake.
Nàge búshì cuòshì.
(Nay-guh boo shr tswoh-shr) 那个不是错事。

It is (there is) a big mistake!
Yǒu dà cuòshì! (You dah tswoh-shr) 有大错事!

92 **Rest** *Xiūxi* *(Show-she)* 休息

I want to rest.
Wǒ yào xiūxi. (Woh yee-ow show-she) 我要休息。

I need to rest.
Wǒ xūyào xiūxi.
(Woh she-yee-ow show-she) 我需要休息。

Can we rest?
Wǒmen néng xiūxi ma?
(Woh-mern nerng show-she mah) 我们能休息吗?

93 Rent Zū *(Joo)* 租

I want to rent a car.
Wǒ yào zū yīliàng chē.
(Woh yee-ow joo ee lee-ahng cher) 我要租一辆车。

What is the rate per day?
Yītiān zūjīn duōshao?
(Yee-tee-an joo jeen dwoh-shou) 一天租金多少?

How do you charge for extra mileage?
Chāochū de lǐchéng zěnme suàn? 超出的里程怎么算?
(Chow-choo der lee-cherng zern-mo swahn)

Does the price include gasoline?
Jiàqian bāokuò qìyóu fèi ma? 价钱包括汽油费吗?
(Jah-chee-an bow-kwoh che-you fay mah)

I want an American car.
Wǒ xiǎng yào yīliàng Měiguó chē.
(Woh shee-ahng yee-ow ee-lee-ahng May-gwoh cher)
我想要一辆美国车。

How many kilometers are included in the basic fee?
Měitiān jīběn de gōnglǐ shù shì duōshao?
(May-tee-an jee-bern der gohng-lee-shoo shr dwoh-shou) 每天基本的公里数是多少?

94 **Bicycle** *Zìxíngchē* *(Jee-sheeng-cher)* 自行车

I want to rent a bicycle.
Wǒ yào zū yīliàng zìxíngchē. 我要租一辆自行车。
(Woh yee-ow joo ee lee-ahng jee-sheeng-cher)

What is the charge per hour?
Yī xiǎoshí duōshao qián?
(Ee she-ow-shr dwoh-shou chee-an) 一小时多少钱?

Do I have to pay in advance?
Yào xiān fù qián ma?
(Yee-ow shee-an foo chee-an ma) 要先付钱吗?

95 **Street** *Jiē* *(Jeh)* 街 / *Jiēdào* *(Jeh-dow)* 街道

alley (narrow street)　　*hútòng (hoo-tohng)* 胡同

What is (the name of) this street?
Zhè shì něi tiáo jiē?
(Jur shr nay-tee-ow jeh) 这是哪条街?

96 **Directions** *Fāngxiàng* *(Fahng-she-ahng)* 方向

How do I get to the _____?
Dào _____ zěnme zǒu?
(Dow _____ zern-mo dzow) 到_____怎么走?

bus station	*qìchē zhàn (chee-cher jahn)*	汽车站
bus stop	*qìchē zhàn (chee-cher jahn)*	汽车站
downtown area	*chéng lǐ (cherng-lee)*	城里
hospital	*yīyuàn (yee-ywahn)*	医院
hotel	*lǚguǎn (lwee-gwahn)*	旅馆

post office	*yóujú* (you-jwee)	邮局
public market	*shìchǎng* (shr-chahng)	市场
railway station	*huǒchē zhàn* (hwoh-cher jahn)	火车站

97 Books *Shū* (Shoo) 书

bookstore   *shūdiàn* (shoo-dee-an) 书店

I'm looking for books about China.
Wǒ yào zhǎo yǒu guānyú Zhōngguó de shū. (Woh
yee-ow jow you gwahn-yuu Johng-gwoh der shoo)
我要找有关于中国的书。

I want to buy some books about China.
Wǒ yào mǎi guānyú Zhōngguó de shū.
(Woh yee-ow my gwahn-yuu Johng-gwoh der shoo)
我要买关于中国的书。

**Where will I find books about the Chinese
language?**
Nǎlǐ yǒu xué Zhōngwén de shū?
(Nah-lee yee-ow shu-eh Johng wern der shoo)
哪里有学中文的书?

Where will I find guidebooks?
Nǎlǐ yǒu lǚyóu xiǎocè?
(Nah-lee you lwee-you shou-tser) 哪里有旅游小册?

Business *Shēngyi* (Sherng-ee) 生意 / *Shēngyè* (shahng-yeh) 生业

advisor	*gùwèn* (goo-wern) 顾问
business person	*shāngrén* (shahng-wren) 商人
business hours	*yíngyè shíjiān* 营业时间 (eeng-yeh shr-jee-an)
capital	*zījīn* (dzu-jeen) 资金
company	*gōngsī* (gohng-suh) 公司
conference meeting	*huìyì* (hway-ee) 会议
conference room	*huìyì shì* (hway-ee shr) 会议室
consulting company	*zīxún gōngsī* 咨询公司 (zhe-sheen gohng-suh)
contract	*hétong* (her-tohng) 合同
director	*dǒngshì* (dohng-shr) 董事
distributor	*xiāoshòu zhě* (shee-ow-show-juh) 销售者
general manager	*zǒngjīnglǐ* (zohng jeeng-lee) 总经理
joint venture	*hézī qǐyè* 合资企业 (her-dzu chee-yeh)
office	*bàngōngshì* (bahn-gohng-shr) 办公室
president (of company)	*zǒngcái* (zohng-tsigh) 总裁
representative	*dàilǐrén* (die-lee-wren) 代理人
vice president (of company)	*fù zǒngcái* (foo zohng-tsigh) 副总裁

foreign-own venture *quánzī yōngyǒu de wàiqǐ*
(chwahn-dzu yohng-you der wie-chee) 全资拥有的外企

Where is your office?
Nǎlǐ shì nǐ de bàngōngshì? (Na-lee shr nee-der bahn-gohng shr) 哪里是你的办公室?

What time does the conference start?
Huìyì jǐdiǎn kāishǐ? (Hway-ee jee-dee-an kigh shr) 会议几点开始?

Great Wall of China *Chángchéng*
(Chahng Cherng) 长城

We would like to see the Great Wall.
Wǒmen xiǎng qù kàn Chángchéng.
(Woh-mern she-ahng chwee kahn Chahng Cherng)
我们想去看长城。

We want to go to the Great Wall.
Wǒmen yào qù Chángchéng. 我们要去长城。
(Woh-mern yee-ow chwee Chahng Cherng)

Please take the most scenic route.
Qǐng zǒu fēngjǐng zuì hǎo de lù. 请走风景最好的路。
(Cheen dzow ferng-jee-in zhui how der loo)

Can you wait for us?
Nǐ néng děng wǒmen ma?
(Nee nerng derng woh-mern mah) 你能等我们吗?

We expect to be back in two hours.
Wǒmen liǎng xiǎoshí jiù huílai. 我们两小时就回来。
(Woh-mern lee-ahng shee-ow-shr jew hway-lie)

100   Goodbye *Zàijiàn* (dzigh jee-an) 再见

Goodbye!
Zàijiàn! (Dzigh jee-an) 再见!

See you later.
Yīhuìr jiàn. (Ee hway-urr jee-an) 一会儿见。

We hope to see you again.
Xīwàng wǒmen zàijiàn miàn. 希望我们再见面。
(She-wahng woh-mern dzigh jee-an-mee-an)

PART 2

Additional Vocabulary

China's Provinces

Ānhuī (Ahn-hway) 安徽

Fújiàn (Foo-jee-ahn) 福建

Gānsù (Gahn-soo) 甘肃

Guǎngdōng (Gwahng-dohng) 广东

Guìzhōu (Gway-joe) 贵州

Hǎinán (High-nahn) 海南

Héběi (Her-bay) 河北

Hēi lóng jiāng (Hay-lohng-jee-ahng) 黑龙江

Hénán (Her-nahn) 河南

Jiāngxī (Jee-ahng-she) 江西

Jílín (Jee-leen) 吉林

Liáoníng (Lee-ow-neeng) 辽宁

Qīnghǎi (Cheeng-high) 青海

Shāndōng (Shahn-dohng) 山东

Shānxī (Shahn-she) 山西

Shǎnxī (Shah-ahn-she) 陕西

Sìchuān (Suh-chwahn) 四川

Yúnnán (Ywun-nahn) 云南

Zhèjiāng (Jur-jee-ahng) 浙江

China's Autonomous Regions

Guǎngxī Zhuàng *(Gwahng-shee Jwahng)* 广西壮
Nèiměnggǔ (Inner Mongolia) *(Nay Merng-goo)*
内蒙古
Níng xià *(Neeng-shee-ah)* 宁夏
Xīzàng (Tibet) *(She-zahng)* 西藏
Xīnjiāng *(Sheen-jee-ahng)* 新疆

Major Cities in China

Ānshān *(Ahn-shahn)* 鞍山
Ānyáng *(ahn-yahng)* 安阳
Àomén *(Ow-mern)* 澳门
Bāotóu *(Bow-toe)* 包头
Běidàihé *(Bay-die-her)* 北戴河
Běihǎi *(Bay-high)* 北海
Běijīng *(Bay-jeeng)* 北京
Chángchūn *(Chahng-chwun)* 长春
Chángshā *(Chahng-shah)* 长沙
Chéngdé *(Chweeng-der)* 承德
Chóngqìng *(Chohng-cheeng)* 重庆
Guǎngzhōu *(Gwahng-joe)* 广州
Dàlǐ *(Dah-lee)* 大里
Dàlián *(Dah-lee-an)* 大连
Dàqìng *(Dah-cheeng)* 大庆
Dūnhuáng *(Dwun-hwahng)* 敦煌
Fóshān *(Fwo-shahn)* 佛山
Fúzhōu *(Foo-joe)* 福州
Guǎngzhōu *(Gwahng-joe)* 广州

Guìyáng (Gway-yahng) 贵阳

Hā'ěrbīn (Hah-urr-bin) 哈尔滨

Huánghé (Hwahng Her) 黄河

Hūhéhàotè (Hoo-her-how-ter) 呼和浩特

Jílín (Jee-leen) 吉林

Jǐnán (Jee-nahn) 济南

Kāifēng (Kigh-ferng) 开封

Kūnmíng (Kwun-meeng) 昆明

Lánzhōu (Lahn-joe) 兰州

Lāsà (Lah-sah) 拉萨

Lùdá (Loo-dah) 陆达

Luòyáng (Lwoh-yahng) 洛阳

Lúshān (Loo Shahn) 庐山

Nánchāng (Nahn-chahng) 南昌

Nánjīng (Nahn-jeeng) 南京

Nánníng (Nahn-neeng) 南宁

Níngbō (Neeng-bwo) 宁波

Níngxià (Neeng-shee-ah) 宁夏

Qīngdǎo (Cheeng-dow) 青岛

Qīnghǎi (Cheeng-high) 青海

Qínhuángdǎo (Cheen-hwahng-dow) 秦皇岛

Quánzhōu (Chwen-joe) 泉州

Qūfù (Chwee-foo) 曲阜

Shànghǎi (Shahng-high) 上海

Shānhǎiguān (Shahn-high-gwahn) 山海关

Shàntóu (Shahn-toe) 汕头

Sháoshān (Shou-shahn) 韶山

Shěnyáng (Shern-Yahng) 沈阳

Shēnzhèn (Shern-zern) 深圳

Tàiyuán (Tie-ywahn) 太原

Tiānjīn *(Tee-an-jeen)* 天津
Tǔlǔfān *(Too-loo-fahn)* 吐鲁番
Wēnzhōu *(Wern-joe)* 温州
Wūlǔmùqí *(Uu-roo-moo chee)* 乌鲁木齐
Wǔhàn *(Woo hahn)* 武汉
Wǔtáishān *(Woo tie shahn)* 五台山
Wúxī *(Woo-she)* 无锡
Xiàmén *(She-ah-mern)* 厦门
Xīān *(She-ahn)* 西安
Xiānggǎng *(Shee-ahng Gahng)* 香港
Xīnjiāng *(Sheen-jee-ahng)* 新疆
Yán'ān *(Yahn-ahn)* 延安
Yángzhōu *(Yahng-joe)* 扬州
Yíxīng *(Ee-sheeng)* 宜兴
Zhènjiāng *(Jun-jee-ahng)* 镇江
Zhèngzhōu *(Juung-joe)* 郑州
Zhūhǎi *(Joo-high)* 珠海

40 Places in China You Mustn't Miss

Here is a list of the 40 most beautiful places in China (Beauty is in the eye of the beholder), in alphabetical order of the name of the province in which they are located. A concise description is also given.

Ānhuī (ahn-hway) 安徽

- **Hongcun Ancient Village** *Hóng cūn (Hohng-tsoon)* 宏村 — a thousand-year old village with a perfect mountain as backdrop.

- **Mount Huangshan** *Ānhuī huángshān (Hwahng Shahn)* 安徽黄山 — a World Heritage Site, considered the most scenic mountain in China.

Fújiàn (Woo-ee Shahn) 福建

- **Mount Wuyi** *Wǔ yí shān* 武夷山 — a World Heritage Site; a mountain with a beautiful, clear river.

- **Xiapu Mudflat** *Xiá pǔ (She-ah Poo)* 霞浦 — the natural beauty of the largest mudflat in China.

Gānsù (gahn-shoo) 甘肃

- **Echoing Sand Mountain and Crescent Lake** *Míngshāshān hé Yuèyáquán (Meeng-shah Shahn her Yu-eh-yah Chwahn)* 鸣沙山和月牙泉 — an heavenly oasis in the middle of the Gobi desert.

Guǎngdōng (Gwahng-dohng) 广东

- **Fortress Towers, Kaiping** *Kāipíngdiāolóu*
  (Kigh-peeng Dee-ow-low) 开平碉楼 — Luxurious
  fortresses with Western influence built in the early
  20th century. Unique in the world.

Guǎngxī (Gwahng-she) 广西

- **Yangshuo** *Yángshuò (Yahng-swoh)* 阳朔 — a
  most well-known tourist destination, Karst at its best.

Guìzhōu (Gway-joe) 贵州

- **Huangguoshu Waterfall** *Huángguǒshù pùbù*
  (Hwahng-gwoh-shoo Poo-boo) 黄果树瀑布 — a
  "77 x 101" meters waterfall in the jungle.

Hǎinán (High-nahn) 海南

- **Guanyin Statue, Nanshan** *Nánshān Hǎishàng
  Guānyīn (Nahn-shahn Hi-shahng Gwahn-eeng)*
  南山海上观音 — the biggest bodhisattva statue in the
  world; built on the sea.

- **Yalong Bay** *Yàlóngwān (Yah-lohng-wahn)* 亚龙湾 — the only world-class tropical beach in China.

Héběi (Her-bay) 河北

- **Chengde Mountain Resort** *Bìshǔ Shānzhuāng (Bee-shoo Shahn-jwahng)* 避暑山庄 — it was used as a summer palace by the Chinese emperors, so it has to be a cool place.

Hēilóngjiāng (Bay-long-jee-ahng) 黑龙江

- **Saint Sophia Cathedral, Harbin** *Shèngsuǒfēiyà Dàjiàotáng (Sherng Swoh-fay-yah Dah-jee-ow-tahng)* 圣索非亚大教堂 — the largest Orthodox church in East and Southeast Asia.

Hénán (Her-nahn) 河南

- **Longtan Valley** *Lóngtán Dàxiágǔ (Lohng-tahn Dah-she-ah-goo)* 龙潭大峡谷 — the No.1 Valley of Narrow Gorges in China.

Húběi (Woo-bay) 湖北

- **One Incense Pillar, Enshi Canyon** *Ēnshī Dàxiágǔ yīzhùxiāng (Ern-shr Dah-she-ah-goo Ee-joo-shee-ahng)* 恩施大峡谷一柱香 — this pillar is 150 meters tall, but only four meters wide. Incredible!

- **Shennongjia** *Shénnóngjià (Shern-nohng Jee-ah)* 神农架 — the only well-preserved sub-tropical forest ecosystem in the world's mid-latitudes.

Húnán (Woo-nahn) 湖南

- **Fenghuang**   *Fènghuáng (Ferng-hwahng)* 凤凰
  — Stilted houses, picture-perfect village.

- **Zhangjiajie**   *Zhāngjiājiè (Jahng-jee-ah Jee-eh)*
  张家界 — the inspiration for the planet Pandora of the
  movie *Avatar*.

Nèi Měnggǔ (Nay Merng-goo) 内蒙古

- **Singing Sand Bay**   *Xiǎngshāwān (Shee-ahng-shah Wahn)* 响沙湾 — the wind here sings in soft
  whispers.

Jiāngsū (Jee-ahng soo) 江苏

- **Brahmā Palace**   *Fàngōng (Fahn-Gohng)* 梵宫
  — Feng shui (geomacy) and Buddhism merged
  together.

Jiāngxī (Jee-ahng she) 江西

- **Mount Lu**   *Lúshān (Loo Shahn)* 庐山 — events
  that changed China happened on this mountain
  frequently.

- **Wuyuan**   *Wùyuán (Woo-Ywahn)* 婺源 — one of
  the most scenic rural places in China.

Jílín (Jee-leen) 吉林

- **Heaven Lake, Changbai Mountain**   *Chángbáishān Tiānchí (Chahng-by-shahn Tee-an-chee)* 长白山天
  池 — the deepest lake in China, inspirational to
  Chinese and Koreans.

Liáoníng (Lee-ow-neeng) 辽宁

- **Benxi Water Cave** *Běnxī Shuǐdòng* (Burn-she Shway-dohng) 本溪水洞 — stalagmites, stalactites and a underground river.

- **Golden Pebble Beach National Resort, Dalian** *Jīnshítān* (Dah-lee-an Jeen-shr-tahn) 金石滩 — ancient rock formations on a picture-perfect golden pebble beach.

Níngxià (Neeng-shee-ah) 宁夏

- **Sand Lake** *Shāhú* (Shah-hoo) 沙湖 — an astonishing wetland flourishing with life in the middle of dry country.

Qīnghǎi (Cheeng-high) 青海

- **Qinghai Lake** *Qīnghǎihú* (Cheeng-high Hoo) 青海湖 — check out Tour de Qinghai, the most famous cycling race in China.

Shǎnxī (Shahn-she) 陕西

- **Xi'an City Wall** *Xīān Chéngqiáng* (She-ahn Churng-chee-ahng) 西安城墙 — a taste of China 1,000 years ago.

Shāndōng (Shahn-dohng) 山东

- **Trestle Bridge, Qingdao** *Qīngdǎo Zhànqiáo* (Cheeng-dow Jee-an-chee-ow) 青岛栈桥 — the pride of this seaside city.

- **Hukou Waterfall** *Húkǒu Pùbù (Hoo-koe Poo-boo)* 壶口瀑布 — it is so famous that it appears on the Chinese 50 Yuan note.

- **Yungang Grottoes** *Yúngāng Shíkū (Ywun-gahng She-koo)* 云冈石窟 — you can spend up to a year in this Buddhism Sanctuary and still have lots to learn.

- **Hailuogou Glacier National Park** *Hǎiluógōu (Hi-lwaw Go)* 海螺沟 — an accessible glacier park, away from civilization.

- **Jiuzhaigou** *Jiǔzhàigōu (Jew-jigh Go)* 九寨沟 — a must-do for both Chinese and international travelers.

- **Potala Palace** *Bùdálāgōng (Boo-dah-lah Gohng)* 布达拉宫 — the crown jewel of Tibet.

Xīnjiāng (Sheen-jee-ahng) 新疆

- **Lake Karakul** *Kālākùlèhú (Kah-lah-koo-ler Hoo)* 喀拉库勒湖—if you survive one the most dangerous roads in the world, you will be rewarded accordingly.

- **Nalati Grassland** *Nuólātí Cǎoyuán (Nah-lah-tee Chow-ywahn)* 那拉提草原 — experience the Kazak culture and best meadow in China.

Yúnnán (Ywun-nahn) 云南

- **Three Pagodas, Dali** *Shěngdàlǐ Chóngshèngsì Sāntǎ (Sherng-Dah-lee Cohng-sherng Suh Sahn-tah)* 省大理崇圣寺三塔 — built in Tang dynasty more than 1,200 years ago, it is still the biggest pagoda in China today.

- **Pudacuo National Park, Shangri-la** *Xiānggélǐlā Pǔdácuò Guójiā Gōngyuán (Shee-ang-geh-lee-la Poo-dah-tswoh Gwoh-jee-ah Gohng-ywahn)* 香格里拉普达措国家公园 — Shangri-la.

Zhèjiāng (Jur-jee-yahng) 浙江

- **Nanxi River** *Nánxī jiāng (Nahn-shee Jee-ahng)* 楠溪江 — like a water-and-ink painting in real life.

- **Thousand Island Lake** *Qiāndǎohú (Chee-an-dow Hoo)* 千岛湖—the Chinese version of Queenstown, and much bigger.

- **Yunhe Rice Terrace** *Yúnhé Tītián (Ywun-her Tee-tee-an)* 云和梯田 — one of the most accessible rice terraces, and certainly one of the best-looking as well.

Famous Places in Beijing

Baiyun (Daoist) Temple *Báiyúnguān (By-ywun Gwahn)* 白云观

Behai Park *Běihǎi Gōngyuán (Bay-high Gohng-ywahn)* 北海公园

Beijing University *Běijǐngdàxué (Bay-jeeng Dah-shway)* 北京大学

Beijing Zoo *Běijǐng Dòngwùyuán (Bay-jeeng Dohng-woo-ywahn)* 北京动物园

Coal Hill *Jǐngshān (Jeeng Shahn)* 景山

Forbidden City *Zǐ jìn Chéng (Dzu-jeen Cherng)* 紫禁城

Front Gate *Qián Mén* (*Chee-an Mern*) 前门

Gate of Supreme Harmony *Tài Hémén* (*Tie Her Mern*) 太和门

Great Hall of the People *Rénmín Dàhuìtáng* (*Wren-meen Dah-hway-tahng*) 人民大会堂

Hall of Perfect Harmony *Zhōng Hédiàn* (*Johng Her Dee-an*) 中和殿

Hall of Preserving Harmony *Bǎo Hédiàn* (*Bow Her Dee-an*) 保和殿

Hall of Supreme Harmony *Tài Hédiàn* (*Tie Her Dee-an*) 太和殿

Hall of Union *Jiāo Tàidiàn* (*Jow Tie Dee-an*) 交泰殿

Imperial Gardens *Yùhuā Yuán* (*Yuu-hwah Ywahn*) 御华园

Imperial Palace *Gù Gōng* (*Goo Gohng*) 故宫

Mao Zedong Memorial Mausoleum *Máozédōng Jìniàntáng* (*Mao jer-dohng Jee-nee-an Tahng*) 毛泽东纪念堂

Marco Polo Bridge *Lúgōuqiáo* (*Loo-go Chee-ow*) 卢沟桥

Museum of Chinese History *Zhōngguó Lìshǐ Bówùguǎn* (*Johng-gwoh lee-shr Bwo-woo Gwahn*) 中国历史博物馆

Museum of the Chinese Revolution *Zhōngguó Ggémìng Bówùguǎn (Johng-gwoh Guh-meeng Bwo-woo Gwahn)* 中国革命博物馆

National Library of China *Zhōngguó Túshūguǎn (Johng-gwoh Tuu-shoo-gwahn)* 中国图书馆

Nationalities Cultural Palace *Mínzú Wénhuàgōng (Meen-joo Wern-hwah Gohng)* 民族文化宫

North Lake Park *Běihǎi Gōngyuán (Bay-high Gohng Ywahn)* 北海公园

Palace of Earthly Tranquility *Kūnníng Gōng (Kwun Neen Gohng)* 坤宁宫

Palace Temple *Yǒnghé Gōng (Yohng-her Gohng)* 永合宫

People's Cultural Park *Rénmín Wénhuà Gōngyuán (Wren-meen Wern-hwah Gohng-ywahn)* 人民文化公园

Summer Palace *Yíhé Yuán (Ee-her Ywahn)* 颐和园

Temple of Heaven *Tiāntán Gōngyuán (Tee-an Tahng Gohng-ywahn)* 天坛公园

Tiananmen Square *Tiānānmén Guǎngchǎng (Tee-an Ahn Mern Gwahng-chahng)* 天安门广场

Xidan Market *Xīdān Shìchǎng (She-dahn Shr-chahng)* 西单市场

Zhongshan Park *Zhōngshān Gōngyuán (Johng-shahn Gohng-ywahn)* 中山公园

Famous Landmarks near Beijing

Great Wall of China *Chángchéng (Chahng Cherng)* 长城

Ming Tombs *Shísān Líng (Shr Sahn Leeng)* 十三陵

Famous Shopping Districts in Beijing

Jiàn'guó Ménwài (Jee-an Gwoh Mern Wigh) 建国门外

Liúlí Chǎng (Leo Lee Chahng) 琉璃场

Qián Mén (Chee-an Mern) 前门

Wángfǔjǐng (Wahng Foo Jeeng) 王府井

Xīdān (She Dahn) 西单

Famous Places in Shanghai

The Bund   *Wàitān Zhōngshānlù (Wigh-tahn Johng-shahn Loo)* 外滩中山路

Fuxing Park   *Fùxīng Gōngyuán (Foo-sheeng Gong Ywahn)* 复兴公园

Jade Buddha Temple   *Yùfósì (Yuu Fwo-suh)* 玉佛寺

Longhua Temple & Pagoda   *Lónghuá miào hé tǎ (Lohng-hwah Mee-ow her Tah)* 龙华庙和塔

Lu Xun Memorial Museum   *Lǔxùn Jìniànguǎn (Loo-sheen Jee-nee-an Gwahn)* 鲁迅纪念馆

Museum of Natural History   *Zìrán Lìshǐ Bówùguǎn (Dzu-rahn Lee-shr Bwo-woo Gwahn)* 自然历史博物馆

Old Town   *Shànghǎi Jiùshì (Shahng-high Jew Shr)* 上海旧市

People's Park-Square   *Rénmín Guǎngchǎng (Wren-meen Gwahng Chahng)* 人民广场

Shanghai Children's Palace   *Shànghǎi Shàonián Gōng (Shahng-high Shou-nee-an Gohng)* 上海少年宫

Shanghai Exhibition Center   *Shànghǎi Zhǎnlǎn Guǎn (Shahng-high Jahn-lahn Gwahn)* 上海展览馆

Shanghai Museum *Shànghǎi Bówùguǎn*
(Shahng-high Bwo-woo Gwahn 上海博物馆)

Sun Yat-sen Residence *Sūnzhōngshān Gùjū*
(Soon Johng-shahn Goo-jwee) 孙中山故居

Tomb of Song Qingling *Sòngqìnglíng Fénmù*
(Sohng Cheeng-leeng Fern-moo) 宋庆龄坟墓

Workers' Cultural Palace *Gōngrén*
Wénhuà Gōng (Gohng-wren Wern-hwah Gohng)
工人文化宫

Xijiao Park *Xījiǎo Gōngyuán* *(She Jow Gohng*
Ywahn) 西角公园

Yu Garden *Yùyuán (Yuu Ywahn)* 豫园

10 Most Well-known
Chinese Personalities

It is always good to know about these people, since they
are often mentioned or cited in conversations in China.

Confucius, or *Kǒngzǐ (Koong-dzu)* 孔子 — a Chinese teacher, politician, philosopher and the founder of
Confucian of the Spring and Autumn period of Chinese
history. He left behind a philosophy that is still much
adopted in modern China.

Sun Tzu *Sūnzi (Soon Dzu)* 孙子 — a great general who
wrote the *Art of War*.

Qín Shǐ Huáng *(Cheen Shr Hwahng)* 秦始皇 — the first Emperor of China; also the King of the state of Qin who conquered all other Warring States and united China into an empire for the first time in Chinese history.

Guan Yu *Guānyǔ* — *(Gwhan Yuu)* 关羽— considered the God of War, was one of the best known Chinese historical figures throughout East Asia.

Li Bai *Lǐbái* *(Lee By)* 李白 — the most famous poet in Chinese history.

Wǔzétiān *(or Wu Tse-t'ian)* **Wǔzétiān** *(Woo Zuh Teean)* 武则天 — the only female emperor in Chinese history.

Yue Fei *Yuèfēi* *(Yu-eh Fay)* 岳飞 — a national hero who represented the essence of Han Chinese culture.

Sun Yat Sen *Sūnzhōngshān* *(Soon Johng Shahn)* 孙中山 — a Chinese revolutionary, first president and founding father of the Republic of China.

Mao Ze Dong/Mao Tse-tung *Máozédōng* *(Mao Jerdohng)* 毛泽东 — a Chinese Communist revolutionary and the founding father of the People's Republic of China.

Ma Yun *Mǎyún* *(Mah Ywun)* 马云 — the richest man in China as of 2015, a household name for being the co-founder of Alibaba, the largest online retail chain in China.

Important Festivals in China

Nowadays Chinese people celebrate both Chinese and Western festivals. The following list some of the most celebrated festivals / holidays in China.

New Year's Day　　*Yuándàn (Ywahn-dahn)* 元旦

Chinese Spring　　*Chūnjié (Choon-jee-eh)* 春节
Festival*

*Common greeting to wish others happiness and prosperity during the lunar new year is:

Xīnnián kuàilè ! (Sheen-nee-an kwie-ler!) 新年快乐!

Happy New Year!
Gōngxǐfācái (gohng-she fah-tsigh) 恭喜发财!　May you be happy and prosperous!

Valentine's Day　　*Qíngrénjié (Cheeng-wren jee-eh)* 情人节

Qingming　　*Qīngmíngjié (Cheeng-meeng*
Festival*　　*jee-eh)* 清明节

*This is a traditional Chinese festival dedicated to tomb-sweeping and paying respect to ancestors.

Children's Day　　*Értóng jié (Uh-tohng-jee-eh)* 儿童节
　　　　　　　　celebrated on June 1st in China.

Mid-Autumn Festival*	*Zhōngqiūjié* *(Johng-chew jee-eh)* 中秋节

*A traditional Chinese festival for family get-togethers and feasts.

Singles' day	*Guānggùnjiē (Gwahng-goon jee-eh)* 光棍节

*A pop culture festival on November 11 (written as 11.11 in Chinese) to celebrate bachelor life. The date is chosen for the connection between singles and the number "1."

Christmas	*Shèngdànjié (Sherng-dahn jee-eh)* 圣诞节

Important Signs

Arrivals   *Jìnguān (Jeen-gwahn)* 进关

Departures   *Chūguān (Choo-gwahn)* 出关

Customs   *Hǎiguān (High-gwahn)* 海关

Bathroom   *Yùshì (Yuu-shr)* 浴室

Occupied (toilet in use)   *Shǐyòng zhōng (Shr-yohng-johng)* 使用中

Alley (narrow street)   *Hútòng (Hoo-tohng)* 胡同

Bicycle Parking   *Cúnchēchù (Tswun-cher choo)* 存车处

Bicycle Parking Zone   *Zìxíngchē cúnchēchù (Dzu-sheeng-cher Tswun-cher-choo)* 自行车存车处

Car Parking Lot   *Tíngchē chǎng (Teeng-cher chang)* 停车场

Closed Door   *Guānmén (Gwahn mern)* 关门

Business Hours	*Yíngyè shíjiān* 营业时间 (Eeng-yeh shr-jee-an)
Bus Stop	*Qìchēzhàn* (Chee-cher jahn) 汽车站
Caution	*Xiǎoxīn* (Shee-ow-sheen) 小心
Closed (business)	*Tíngzhǐ yíngyè* (Teeng-jr-eeng-yeh) 停止营业 / *Guānmén* (Gwahn-mern) 关门
Danger	*Wēixiǎn* (Way-shee-an) 危险
Emergency Exit	*Jǐnjí chūkǒu* (Jeen-jee Choo-koe) 紧急出口 / *Tàipíng mén* (Tie-peeng mern) 太平门
Entrance	*Rùkǒu* (Roo-koe) 入口
Exit	*Chūkǒu* (Choo-koe) 出口
Do Not Enter	*Bùxǔ jìnrù* (Boo-shee Jeen-roo) 不许进入
Don't Touch	*Wù chù* (Woo-choo) 勿触 / *Wù mō* (Woo-mwo) 勿摸
Drinking Water	*Yǐnyòngshuǐ* (Eeng-yohng shway) 饮用水
Elevator	*Diàntī* (Dee-an-tee) 电梯
Employees Only	*Xián rén miǎn rù* 闲人免入 (Shee-an-wren mee-an- roo)
First Aid	*Jíjiù* (Jee Jeo) 急救
Forbidden	*Jìnzhǐ* (Jeen-jr) 禁止
Hospital	*Yīyuàn* (Ee-ywahn) 医院
Information	*Tōngzhī* (Tohng-jr) 通知
Information Desk	*Wènxùn tái* (Wern-sheen tai) 问讯台

Information Office	*Wènxùn chù* *(Wern-sheen choo)* 问讯处
Keep Out	*Qǐng wù rù nèi* 请勿入内 *(Cheeng-woo roo-nay)*
Ladies' Room	*Nǔ cèsuǒ* *(Nwee tser-swoh)* 女厕所
Left Luggage Storage	*Xíngli jìcún chù* 行李寄存处 *(Sheeng-lee jee-tswun choo)*
Luggage Lockers	*Xíngli guì* *(Sheeng-lee gway)* 行李柜
Main Street	*Dàjiē (Dah-jee-eh)* 大街
Men's Room	*Nán cèsuǒ (Nahn tser-swoh)* 男厕所
Non-potable Water	*Fēi yǐnyòngshuǐ (Fay eeng-yoong shway)* 非饮用水
No Entrance / No Entry	*Jìnzhǐ rù nèi (Jeen-jr roo-nay)* 禁止入内
No Parking	*Bùxǔ tíngchē (Boo she-teeng-cher)* 不许停车
No Picture Taking	*Qǐng wù pāizhào (Cheeng woo pie-jow)* 请勿拍照
No Smoking	*Qǐng wù xīyān (Cheeng woo she-yahn)* 请勿吸烟
No Spitting	*Qǐng wù tǔtán (Cheeng woo too-tahn)* 请勿吐痰
No Trespassing	*Bùzhǔn rù nèi (Boo joon roo-nay)* 不准入内
Open (for business)	*Yíngyè (Eeng-yeh)* 营业
Open Door	*Kāimén (Kigh mern)* 开门

Please Don't Touch	*Qǐng wù dòngshǒu (Cheeng woo dohng-show)* 请勿动手
Please Line Up	*Qǐng páiduì (Cheeng pie-dway)* 请排队
Police	*Jǐngchá (Jeeng-chah)* 警察
Public Bath	*Yùchí (Yuu Chr)* 浴池
Public Telephone	*Gōngyòng diànhuà (Gohng-yohng dee- an-hwah)* 公用电话
Public Toilet	*Gōngyòng cèsuǒ (Gohng-yohng tser- swoh)* 公用厕所
Pull	*Lā (Lah)* 拉
Push	*Tuī (Tway)* 推
Reserved	*Yùyuē (Yuu-yuu-eh)* 预约
Self-Service	*Zìzhù (Dzu-joo)* 自助
Smoking Permitted	*Kěyǐ xīyān (Kuh-ee she-yahn)* 可以吸烟
Sold Out	*Quán mǎn (Chwahn mahn)* 全满
Full House	*Kè mǎn (Ker mahn)* 客满
Ticket Office	*Shòupiào chù (Show-pee-ow choo)* 售票处
Toilet	*Cèsuǒ (Tser-swoh)* 厕所
Vacancy	*Yǒu kōng fáng (You kohng fahng)* 有空房
Waiting Room	*Xiūxī shì (Sheo-she shr)* 休息室
Welcome	*Huānyíng guānglín (Hwahn-eeng gwahng-leen)* 欢迎光临
Admission Free	*Miǎnfèi rùchǎng (Mee-an-fay roo-chahng)* 免费入场

Other Countries in Chinese

Australia	*Àodàlìyà (Ah-oh-dah-lee-ah)*	澳大利亚
Canada	*Jiānádà (Jya-nah-dah)*	加拿大
France	*Fǎguó (Fah-gwoh)*	法国
Germany	*Déguó (Duh-gwoh)*	德国
Great Britain	*Yīngguó (Eeng-gwoh)*	英国
India	*Yìndù (Een-doo)*	印度
Italy	*Yìdàlì (Ee-dah-lee)*	意大利
Japan	*Rìběn (Ree-bern)*	日本
(North) Korea	*Cháoxiǎn (Chow-she-an)*	朝鲜
(South) Korea	*Hánguó (Hang-gwoh)*	韩国
New Zealand	*Niǔxīlán (New She-lahn)*	纽西兰
Pakistan	*Bājīsītǎn (Bah-jee-she-tahn)*	巴基斯坦
Spain	*Xībānyá (She-bahn-yah)*	西班牙
United States	*Měiguó (May-gwoh)*	美国

Opposites

big / small	*dà / xiǎo (dah / shaow)*	大／小
heavy / light	*zhòng / qīng (johng / cheeng)*	重／轻
long / short	*cháng / duǎn (chahng / dwan)*	长／短
good / bad	*hǎo / huài (how / hwai)*	好／坏
cheap / expensive	*piányi / guì (pee-an-ee / gwee)*	便宜／贵
easy / difficult	*róngyì / nán (rohng ee / nahn)*	容易／难
true / false	*zhēn / jiǎ (jun / jah)*	真／假
quick / slow	*kuài / màn (kwie / mahn)*	快／慢
left / right	*zuǒ / yòu (zwoh / you)*	左／右
early / late	*zǎo / wǎn (dzow / wahn)*	早／晚
old / young	*lǎo / shào (lao / shaow)*	老／少
full / empty	*mǎn / kōng (mahn / kohng)*	满／空
safe / dangerous	*ānquán / wēixiǎn (ahn-chwan / way-shee-an)*	安全／危险
quiet / noisy	*ānjìng / chǎonào (ahn-jeen / chow-now)*	安静／吵闹
inside / outside	*lǐbian / wàibian (lee-bee-an / wie-bee-an)*	里边／外边
first / last	*xiān / hòu (shee-an / hoh)*	先／后
before / after	*yǐqián / yǐhòu (ee-chee-an / ee-hoh)*	以前／以后

Words A to Z

3D movie *sāndi diànyǐng (sahn-dee dee-an eeng)* 3D电影

[A]

abacus *suànpán (swahn-pahn)* 算盘

abalone *bàoyú (bow-yuu)* 鲍鱼

Action (movie) *Dòngzuò piàn (doong zwoh pee-an)* 动作片

abroad *guówài (gwoh-wigh)* 国外

accept *jiēshòu (jay show)* 接受

accurate *zhǔnquè (joon-chueh)* 准确

actor *yǎnyuán (yahn-ywahn)* 演员

acupuncture *zhēnjiǔ (jun-jeo)* 针灸

adaptor plug *zhuǎnjiē qì (jwahn-jee-eh chee)* 转接器

address *dìzhǐ (dee-jr)* 地址

admission *rùchǎng (roo-chahng)* 入场

adult *dàren (dah-wren)* 大人

aerobics *jiànměi cāo (jee-an-may tsow)* 健美操

after (prep.) *guò (gwoh)* 过

again *zài (zigh)* 再

against *fǎnduì (fahn dway)* 反对

agree *tóngyì (tohng-ee)* 同意

agriculture *nóngyè (nohng-yeh)* 农业

AIDS *Àizībìng (aye-dzu beeng)* 爱滋病

air *kōngqì (kohng-chee)* 空气

air-conditioner	*kōngtiáo jī (kohng-tow-jee)* 空调机
airconditioning	*kōngtiáo (kohng-tee-ow)* 空调
airline (company)	*hángkōng gōngsī (hahng-kohng gohng-suh)* 航空公司
airline hostess	*kōngzhōng xiǎojie (kohng-johng shiaow-jah)* 空中小姐
airline ticket	*fēijī piào (fay-jee pee-ow)* 飞机票
air pollution	*kōngqì wūrǎn (koong-chee woo-rahn)* 空气污染
airsick	*yūn jī (ywun-jee)* 晕机
alarm clock	*nàozhōng (now johng)* 闹钟
alcohol	*jiǔ (jeo)* 酒
a little	*yīdiǎn (ee-dee-an)* 一点
all	*quánbù (chwahn boo)* 全部
allergy	*guòmǐn (gwoh-meen)* 过敏
alley	*hútòng (hoo-tohng)* 胡同
altitude	*hǎibá (high-bah)* 海拔
ambassador	*dàshǐ (dah-shr)* 大使
amount, total	*zǒng'é (zohng urr)* 总额
amusing, fun	*hǎowán (how-wahn)* 好玩
Android phone	*ānzhuó shǒujī (ahn-jwoh show-jee)* 安卓手机
ancient	*gǔdài de (goo-die-duh)* 古代的
angry	*shēngqì (sherng-chee)* 生气
animal	*dòngwù (dohng-woo)* 动物
anniversary	*zhōunián jìniàn (joe-nee-an jee-nee-an)* 周年纪念
announcement	*gōnggào (gohng gaw)* 公告

answer	*huídá* (hway-dah)	回答
antibiotics	*kàngshēngsù* (kahng-sherng-soo)	抗生素
apartment	*dānyuán fáng* (dahn-ywahn fahng)	单元房
appendicitis	*mángchángyán* (mahng chahng yahn)	盲肠炎
appetizer	*lěngpán* (lerng-pahn)	冷盘
applaud	*pāishǒu* (pie-show)	拍手
appliance	*diànqì* (dee-an-chee)	电器
application	*shēnqǐng* (sherng-cheeng)	申请
application form	*shēnqǐng biǎo* (sherng-cheeng bow)	申请表
appointment	*yuēhuì* (yway-hway)	约会
appreciate	*xīnshǎng* (sheen-shahng)	欣赏
architecture	*jiànzhù* (jee-an-joo)	建筑
area (district)	*yīdài* (ee-die)	一带
army	*jūnduì* (jwin-dway)	军队
arrival card	*rùjìng kǎ* (roo-jeeng-kah)	入境卡
arrive	*dàodá* (dow-dah)	到达
art	*yìshù* (ee-shoo) 艺术 / *měishù* (may-shoo)	美术
art gallery	*huàláng* (hwah-lahng)	画廊
artist	*yìshùjiā* (ee-shoo-jah)	艺术家
art museum	*měishùguǎn* (may-shoo gwahn)	美术馆
arts & crafts	*gōngyì měishù* (gohng-ee may-shoo)	工艺美术
Asia	*Yàzhōu* (Yah-joe)	亚洲
ask	*wèn* (wern)	问

assignment	*gōngzuò (gohng-zwoh)*	工作
assist, help	*bāngzhù (bahng-joo)*	帮助
asthma	*qìchuǎnbìng (chee-chwahn beeng)*	气喘病
athletics	*yùndòng (ywun-dohng)*	运动
attorney	*lǜshī (lwee-shr)*	律师
attractive	*xīyǐn rén (she-een-wren)*	吸引人
audience	*guānzhòng (gwahn-johng)*	观众
auditorium	*lǐtáng (lee-tahng)*	礼堂
aunt	*gūgu (goo-goo)*	姑姑
authentic	*kěkào (ker-kow)*	可靠
author	*zuòzhě (zwoh-juh)*	作者
authorize	*shòuquán (show-chwahn)*	授权
automatic	*zìdòng (dzu-dohng)*	自动
automobile	*qìchē (chee-cher)*	汽车
avenue	*dàjiē (dah-jeh)*	大街
average	*píngjūn (peeng-jwin)*	平均
awake, wake up	*huànxǐng (hwahng-sheeng)*	唤醒

[B]

baby	*yīngér (eeng-urr)*	婴儿
baby food	*yīngér shípǐn (eeng-urr shr-peen)*	婴儿食品
bachelor	*dānshēn hàn (dahn-shern-hahn)*	单身汉
back door	*hòumén (hoe mern)*	后门
back yard	*hòuyuàn (hoe ywahn)*	后院
bad (quality)	*chà (chah)*	差
badminton	*yǔmáoqiú (yuu-mao chew)*	羽毛球

bag	*dàizi (die-dzu)* 袋子
baggage	*xíngli (sheeng-lee)* 行李
baggage cart	*xíngli chē (sheeng-lee cher)* 行李车
baggage check	*xíngli tuōyùn dān (sheeng-lee twoh-ywun-dahn)* 行李托运单
baggage claim	*xíngli tīng (sheeng-lee teeng)* 行李厅
baggage tag	*xíngli pái (sheeng-lee pie)* 行李牌
bakery	*miànbāo diàn (me-an-bow dee-an)* 面包店
ball	*qiú (cheo)* 球
ball game	*qiúsài (cheo sigh)* 球赛
ballpoint pen	*yuánzhūbǐ (ywahn-joo bee)* 圆珠笔
ballroom	*wǔtīng (woo-teeng)* 舞厅
bamboo	*zhúzi (joo-dzu)* 竹子
bamboo shoots	*zhúsǔn (joo soon)* 竹笋
banana	*xiāngjiāo (she-ahng-jow)* 香蕉
band (musical)	*yuèduì (yway-dway)* 乐队
bandage	*bēngdài (bung-die)* 绷带
band-aid	*zhǐxuè jiāobù (jr-shway jee-ow-boo)* 止血胶布
bank	*yínháng (een-hahng)* 银行
banquet	*yànhuì (yahn-hway)* 宴会
banquet room	*yànhuì tīng (yahn-hway teeng)* 宴会厅
bar (drinking)	*jiǔbā (jeo-bah)* 酒吧
barbecue	*kǎo (kow)* 烤
barter	*yǐ huò yì huò (ee-hwoh ee-hwoh)* 以货易货

baseball	*bàngqiú (bahng-cheo)* 棒球
basement	*dìxiàshì (dee-she-ah-shr)* 地下室
basketball	*lánqiú (lahn-cheo)* 篮球
basketball game	*lánqiú sài (lahn-cheo sigh)* 篮球赛
bathe	*xǐzǎo (she-zow)* 洗澡
bathing beach	*yùchǎng (yuu chahng)* 浴场
bathing suit	*yóuyǒngyī (you-yohng-ee)* 游泳衣
bathrobe	*yùyī (yuu yee)* 浴衣
bathroom (bath)	*yùshì (yuu-shr)* 浴室
bathroom (toilet)	*cèsuǒ (tser-swoh)* 厕所
bath towel	*xǐzǎo máojīn (she-zow mao-jeen)* 洗澡毛巾
bathtub	*zǎo pén (zow-pern)* 澡盆 / *yùgāng (yuu-gahng)* 浴缸
batteries	*diànchí (dee-an-chr)* 电池
bay	*hǎiwān (high-wahn)* 海湾
beach	*hǎitān (high-tahn)* 海滩
bean curd	*dòufu (doe-foo)* 豆腐
beard	*húzi (hoo-dzu)* 胡子
beat, win	*yíng (eeng)* 赢
beautiful	*piàoliang (pee-ow-lee-ahng)* 漂亮
beauty (natural)	*zìrán měi (dzu-rahn-may)* 自然美
beauty salon	*fàláng (fah lahng)* 发廊
bed	*chuáng (chwahng)* 床
bedroom	*wòshì (woh-shr)* 卧室 / *wòfáng (woh-fahng)* 卧房
beef	*niúròu (new-roe)* 牛肉
beefsteak	*niúpái (new pie)* 牛排
beer	*píjiǔ (pee jeo)* 啤酒

before	*yǐqián (ee-chee-an)* 以前	
bell (door)	*líng (leeng)* 铃	
bell captain	*xíngli lǐngbān (sheeng-lee leeng-bahn)* 行李领班	
belt	*yāodài (yee-ow-die)* 腰带	
best	*zuìhǎo (zway-how)* 最好	
better	*bǐjiào hǎo (bee-jow-how)* 比较好	
beverage	*yǐnliào (een-lee-ow)* 饮料	
big, large, great	*dà (dah)* 大	
birds	*niǎo (nee-ow)* 鸟	
birth control	*jiéyù (jeh-yuu)* 节育	
birthday	*shēngrì (sherng-rr)* 生日	
biscuit	*bǐnggān (beeng-gahn)* 饼干	
black	*hēi (hay)* 黑	
blanket	*tǎnzi (tahn-dzu)* 毯子	
bleed	*liúxuè (lew-shway)* 流血	
blonde	*jīnfà (jeen-fah)* 金发	
blister	*pào (pow)* 疱	
blood-pressure	*xuèyā (shway-yah)* 血压	
blood type	*xuèxíng (shway sheeng)* 血型	
blue	*lán (lahn)* 蓝	
Bluetooth	*lányá (lahn-yah)* 蓝牙	
boarding pass	*dēngjīpái (derng-jee pei)* 登机牌	
boat	*chuán (chwahn)* 船	
body (human)	*shēntǐ (shern-tee)* 身体	
body temperature	*tǐwēn (tee-wern)* 体温	
boil (verb)	*zhǔ (joo)* 煮	
boiled egg	*zhǔ jīdàn (joo jee-dahn)* 煮鸡蛋	

boiled water	*kāishuǐ (kigh shway)* 开水	
bon voyage	*yīlùshùnfēng (ee-loo-shwern-ferng)* 一路顺风	
bookkeeper	*kuàijì (kwie-jee)* 会计	
booth	*tíng (teeng)* 亭	
boots	*xuēzi (shway-dzu)* 靴子	
border	*biānjiè (bee-an-jay)* 边界	
borrow	*jiè (jay)* 借	
boss	*lǎobǎn (lao-bahn)* 老板	
bottle	*píng (peeng)* 瓶	
bottle opener	*kāipíng qì (kigh peeng-chee)* 开瓶器	
boulevard	*dàdào (dah-dow)* 大道	
bowl	*wǎn (wahn)* 碗	
box	*hézi (her-dzu)* 盒子	
boxing	*quánjī (chwahn-jee)* 拳击	
boy	*nánhái (nahn-high-urr)* 男孩	
boyfriend	*nánpéngyou (nahn perng-you)* 男朋友	
bra	*rǔzhào (roo-jow)* 乳罩	
branch office	*fēnbù (fern boo)* 分部	
brand	*shāngbiāo (shahng-bee-ow)* 商标	
bread	*miànbāo (mee-an-bow)* 面包	
breast	*rǔfáng (roo-fahng)* 乳房	
bride	*xīnniáng (sheen-nee-ahng)* 新娘	
bridegroom	*xīnláng (sheen-lahng)* 新郎	
bridge	*qiáo (chow)* 桥	
brother	*xiōngdì (she-ong-dee)* 兄弟	
Buddhism	*Fójiào (Fwo-jow)* 佛教	
Buddhist	*Fójiàotú (Fwo-jow too)* 佛教徒	

budget	*yùsuàn (yuuswahn)* 预算	
buffet	*zìzhù cān (dzu-joo-tsahn)* 自助餐	
buffet dinner	*zìzhù wǎncān (dzu-joo wahn-tsahn)* 自助晚餐	
buffet lunch	*zìzhù wǔcān (dzu-joo woo-tsahn)* 自助午餐	
bullet train	*dòngchē (doong-cher)* 动车	
building	*lóufáng (low-fahng)* 楼房	
businessperson	*shāngrén (shahng-wren)* 商人	
busy	*máng (mahng)* 忙	
butter	*huángyóu (hwahng-yoe)* 黄油	

[C]

cabbage	*juǎnxīncài (jwen sheen tsigh)* 卷心菜
cabin	*kècāng (ker-tsahng)* 客仓
cable television	*bìlù diànshì (bee-loo dee-an-shr)* 闭路电视
café	*kāfēi guǎn (kah-fay-gwahn)* 咖啡馆
cafeteria	*shítáng (shr-tahng)* 食堂
calculator	*jìsuànjī (jee-swahn-jee)* 计算机
canal	*yùnhé (ywun-her)* 运河
cancel	*qǔxiāo (chwee-she-ow)* 取消
capital (city)	*shǒudū (show-doo)* 首都
Cappuccino	*kǎbùqínuò (kah-boo-chee-nwoh)* 卡布奇诺
cash	*xiànjīn (shee-an-jeen)* 现金
cashier	*chūnà (choo-nah)* 出纳
casual	*suíbiàn (sway-bee-an)* 随便
cell phone	*shǒujī (show-jee)* 手机

centigrade	*shèshì (sher-shr)* 摄氏
central	*zhōngyāng (johng-yahng)* 中央
cereal	*màipiàn (my-pee-an)* 麦片
ceremony	*diǎnlǐ (dee-an-lee)* 典礼
chair	*yǐzi (ee-dzu)* 椅子
change (money)	*língqián (leeng-chee-an)* 零钱
changing money	*duìhuàn (dway-hwahn)* 兑换
cheap	*piányi (pee-an-ee)* 便宜
check (noun)	*zhīpiào (jr-pee-ow)* 支票
check in	*rù zhù (roo-joo)* 入住
check in (at airport)	*bàn chéng shǒuxù (bahn cherng show-shee)* 办程手续
check out (hotel)	*tuìfáng (tway-fahng)* 退房
cheers	*Gānbēi! (Gahn-bay)* 干杯!
chef's special	*zhǔchú tècān (joo-choo ter-tsahn)* 主厨特餐
cheongsam (dress)	*qípáo (chee-pow)* 旗袍
child	*háizi (high-dzu)* 孩子
Chinese movie	*Zhōngguó diànyǐng (Johng gwoh dee-an eeng)* 中国电影
Chinese Spring Festival	*Chūnjié (Choon-jee-eh)* 春节
chocolate	*qiǎokèlì (chiao-ker-lee)* 巧克力
chopsticks	*kuàizi (kwie-dzu)* 筷子
Christmas	*Shèngdànjié (Sherng-dahn jee-eh)* 圣诞节
church	*jiàotáng (jow-tahng)* 教堂

city, town	*chéngshì (cherng-shr)* 城市
city map	*chéngshì jiāotōngtú (cherng-shr jow-tohng too)* 城市交通图
classmate	*tóngxué (tohng-shway)* 同学
climb (a hill)	*pá shān (pah-shahn)* 爬山
cloakroom	*yīmàojiān (ee-mao-jee-an)* 衣帽间
closing time	*guānmén (gwahn mern)* 关门
clothing	*yīfu (ee-foo)* 衣服
club (recreational)	*jùlèbù (jwee-ler-boo)* 俱乐部
coach, bus	*chángtú qìchē (chahng-too-chee-cher)* 长途汽车
coat	*dàyī (dah-ee)* 大衣
Coca-cola (coke)	*kěkǒu kělè (ker-koe ker-ler)* 可口可乐
cocktail	*jīwěijiǔ (jee-way-jew)* 鸡尾酒
cocktail party	*jīwěijiǔ huì (jee-way-jew-hway)* 鸡尾酒会
cold dishes	*lěngpán (lerng-pahn)* 冷盘
cold drink	*lěngyǐn (lerng een)* 冷饮
color	*yánsè (yahn-suh)* 颜色
comedy	*xìjù (see-jwee)* 戏剧
comfortable	*shūfu (shoo-foo)* 舒服
communist party	*Gòngchǎndǎng (Gohng-chahng-dahng)* 共产党
concert	*yīnyuè huì (een-yway-hway)* 音乐会
condensed milk	*liànrǔ (lee-an-roo)* 炼乳
condom	*bìyùn tào (bee-yuun-tao)* 避孕套

Confucius	*Kǒngzǐ (Koong-dzu)* 孔子	
congratulations	*gōngxǐ (gohng-see)* 恭喜	
contact lenses	*yǐnxíng yǎnjìng (yeen-sheeng yahn-jeeng)* 隐形眼镜	
corner (street)	*guǎi jiǎo (gwie-jow)* 拐角	
correct	*duì (dway)* 对	
counter (sales)	*guìtái (gway-tie)* 柜台	
counter (service)	*fúwùtái (foo-woo-tie)* 服务台	
country (nation)	*guójiā (gwoh-jah)* 国家	
countryside	*nóngcūn (nohng-tswun)* 农村	
cream	*nǎiyóu (nigh-you)* 奶油	
crowd	*rénqún (wren-chween)* 人群	
crowded	*yōngjǐ (yohng-jee)* 拥挤	
cultural	*wénhuà de (wern-hwah der)* 文化的	
cultural exchange	*wénhuà jiāoliú (wern-hwah jee-ow lew)* 文化交流	
culture	*wénhuà (wern-hwah)* 文化	
currency	*huòbì (hwoh-bee)* 货币	
custom (way)	*fēngsú (foong-soo)* 风俗	
customer	*gùkè (goo-ker)* 顾客	
Customs	*hǎiguān (High-gwahn)* 海关	
Customs tariff	*guānshuì (Gwahn-shway)* 关税	
[D]		
dad	*bàba (bah-bah)* 爸爸	
daily	*měitiān (may-tee-an)* 每天	
daily paper	*rìbào (rr bow)* 日报	
dance (verb)	*tiàowǔ (tee-ow-woo)* 跳舞	

dance hall	*wǔtīng* (woo teeng) 舞厅
dance party	*wǔhuì* (woo hway) 舞会
date (courting)	*yuēhuì* (ywway-hway) 约会
declare	*shēnbào* (shern-bow) 申报
degree (college)	*xuéwèi* (shway-way) 学位
delicatessen	*shúshí diàn* (shoo-shr dee-an) 熟食店
democracy	*mínzhǔ* (meen-joo) 民主
demonstration	*shìwēi* (shr-way) 示威
department	*bù* (boo) 部
departure	*chūfā* (chwee-fah) 出发
departure card	*chūjìng kǎ* (choo-jeeng-kah) 出境卡
deposit (money)	*yājīn* (yah-jeen) 押金
dessert	*tiánpǐn* (tee-an-peen) 甜品
dictionary	*zìdiǎn* (dzu-dee-an) 字典
diplomat	*wàijiāo jiā* (weigh-jee-ow-jah) 外交家
disabled person	*cánzhàng rénshì* (tsahnzahng-wren-shr) 残障人士
disco	*dísīgētīng* (dee-ss-ger teeng) 迪斯歌厅
discount	*zhékòu* (juh-koe) 折扣
divorce	*líhūn* (lee-hwun) 离婚
domestic	*guónèi* (gwoh-nay) 国内
dormitory	*sùshè* (soo-sher) 宿舍
double room	*shuāngrén fáng* (shwahng-wren fahng) 双人房
downtown	*shì zhōngxīn* (shr-johng-sheen) 市中心

draft beer	*chā pí (jah pee)* 喳啤	
Dragon Boat Festival	*Duānwǔjié (Dwahn Woo Jeh)* 端午节	
dragon boat race	*lóngzhōu bǐsài (lohng joe bee-sigh)* 龙舟比赛	
dress (noun)	*yīfu (ee-foo)* 衣服	
drinking straw	*xīguǎn (she-gwahn)* 吸管	
driver	*sījǐ (suh-jee)* 司机	
driver's license	*jiàshǐ zhízhào (jah-shr jr-chow)* 驾驶执照	
drugstore	*yàodiàn (yow-dee-an)* 药店	
drunk, tipsy	*zuì (zway)* 醉	
duck	*yā (yah)* 鸭	
dust	*huīchén (hway-chern)* 灰尘	
duty (customs)	*shuì (shway)* 税	
duty free	*miǎn shuì (mee-an-shway)* 免税	

[E]

early	*zǎo (zow)* 早	
earphone	*ěrjī (urr-jee)* 耳机	
earthquake	*dìzhèn (dee-jun)* 地震	
east	*dōng (dohng)* 东	
East China Sea	*Dōng Hǎi (Dohng High)* 东海	
economy	*jīngjì (jeeng-jee)* 经济	
editor	*biānjí (bee-an-jee)* 编辑	
election	*xuǎnjǔ (shwen-jwee)* 选举	
electric plug	*diàn chātóu (dee-an chah-toe)* 电插头	
elevator	*diàntī (dee-an-tee)* 电梯	

e-mail	*diànzǐ yóuxiāng (dee-an-dzu you-shee-ahng)* 电子邮箱
emergency room	*jízhěn shì (jee-jun shr)* 急诊室
English language	*Yīngwén (Eeng-wern)* 英文
entrance	*rùkǒu (roo-koe)* 入口
entry visa	*rùjìng qiānzhèng (roo-jeeng chee-an-zhehng)* 入境签证
error	*cuòwù (tswoh-woo)* 错误
escalator	*zìdòng fútī (dzu-dohng-foo-tee)* 自动扶梯
Espresso	*Yìdàlì nóng kāfēi (ee-dah-lee nohng kah-fay)* 意大利浓咖啡
Europe	*Ōuzhōu (Oh-joe)* 欧洲
European (person)	*Ōuzhōurén (Oh-joe-wren)* 欧洲人
evening	*wǎnshang (wahn-shahng)* 晚上
evening dress	*wǎn lǐfú (wahn lee-foo)* 晚礼服
evening party	*wǎnhuì (wahn hway)* 晚会
exhausted	*lèihuài le (lay-hwie-luh)* 累坏了
exhibition	*zhǎnlǎn huì (jahn-lahn-hway)* 展览会
exhibition hall	*zhǎnlǎn guǎn (jahn-lahn gwahn)* 展览馆
exit	*chūkǒu (choo-koe)* 出口
expenses	*fèiyòng (fay-yohng)* 费用
expensive	*guì (gway)* 贵
expert	*shúliàn (shuu-lee-an)* 熟练

extension cord	*jiēcháng diànxiàn* (jeh-chang dee-an-she-an) 接长电线	
eyedrops	*yǎn yàoshuǐ* (yahn-yow-shway) 眼药水	
eyeglasses	*yǎnjìng* (yahn-jeeng) 眼镜	

[F]

face	*liǎn* (lee-an) 脸
Facebook	*liǎnshū* (lee-an-shoo) 脸书
factory	*gōngchǎng* (gohng-chahng) 工厂
Fahrenheit	*Huáshì* (hwah-shr) 华氏
faint	*tóu hūn* (toe-ywun) 头昏
fake	*màopái* (mao-pie) 冒牌
fall (verb)	*shuāidǎo* (shoo-ai-dow) 摔倒
family	*jiā* (jah) 家
family members	*qīnrén* (cheen wren) 亲人
famous	*yǒumíng* (you-meeng) 有名
famous dish	*míng cài* (meeng tsigh) 名菜
far	*yuǎn* (ywahn) 远
farm	*nóngchǎng* (nohng-chahng) 农场
farmer	*nóngfū* (nohng-foo) 农夫
fast food	*kuàicān* (kwie-tsahn) 快餐
fashion	*shímáo* (shr-mao) 时髦
fault	*cuò* (tswoh) 错
fee, expense	*fèiyòng* (fay-yohng) 费用
female	*nǚ* (nwee) 女
festival	*jiérì* (jeer-rr) 节日
fiancé	*wèihūnfū* (way-hwun-foo) 未婚夫

fine, penalty	*fákuǎn (fah-kwahn)*	罚款
fire (conflagration)	*huǒzāi (hwoh-zigh)*	火灾
fire alarm	*huǒ jǐng (hwoh jeeng)*	火警
fire escape	*ānquán tī (ahn-chwahn tee)*	安全梯
fire exit	*tàipíng mén (tie-peeng mern)*	太平门
firecracker	*biānpào (bee-an pow)*	鞭炮
first-aid kit	*jíjiù xiāng (jee jeo she-ahng)*	急救箱
first-class	*tóuděng (toe-derng)*	头等
fish	*yú (yuu)*	鱼
flag	*qízi (chee-dzu)*	旗子
flashlight	*shǒudiàntǒng (show-dee-an-toong)*	手电筒
flood	*shuǐzāi (shway-zigh)*	水灾
flowers	*huār (hwah-urr)*	花儿
flower shop	*huādiàn (hwah dee-an)*	花店
folk dance	*mínjiān wǔdǎo (meen-jee-an woo-dow)*	民间舞蹈
folk music	*mínjiān yīnyuè (meen-jee-an een-yway)*	民间音乐
food poisoning	*shíwù zhòngdú (shr-woo johng-doo)*	食物中毒
foreign	*wàiguó de (wigh-gwoh-der)*	外国的
foreign exchange	*wàihuì (wigh-hway)*	外汇
foreign guest	*wàibīn (wigh been)*	外宾
forest	*shùlín (shoo-leen)*	树林
free (cost)	*miǎnfèi (mee-an-fay)*	免费
free (time)	*yǒu kòng (you kohng)*	有空

free trade zone   *zìyóu màoyì (dzu-you mao-ee-choo)*
自由贸易

freezing   *bīngdòng (beeng-doong)* 冰冻

French cuisine   *Fǎguó cài (fah-gwoh tsigh)* 法国菜

French fries   *zhá shǔtiáo (zah shoo-tee-ow)*
炸薯条

frozen food   *lěngcáng shípǐn (lerng-tsahng*
shr-peen) 冷藏食品

fruit   *shuǐguǒ (shway-gwoh)* 水果

fruit juice   *guǒzhī (gwoh-jr)* 果汁

fruit store   *shuǐguǒ diàn (shway-gwoh dee-an)*
水果店

full   *mǎn le (mahn-ler)* 满了

full stomach   *bǎo (bow)* 饱

fuse (noun)   *bǎoxiǎnsī (bow-shee-an-suh)*
保险丝

[G]

gamble   *dǔbó (doo-bwoh)* 赌博

gambling house   *dǔchǎng (doo chahng)* 赌场

game, match   *qiúsài (cheo-sigh)* 球赛

gangster (movie)   *jǐngfěi piàn (jeeng fay pee-an)*
警匪片

garbage   *lājī (lah-jee)* 垃圾

garden   *huāyuán (hwah-ywahn)* 花园

garlic   *suàn (swahn)* 蒜

gasoline   *qìyóu (chee-you)* 汽油

gasoline station   *jiāyóuzhàn (jah-you jahn)* 加油站

German   *Déwén (Duh-wern)* 德文

ghost (movie)   *guǐ piàn (gway pee-an)* 鬼片

ginseng   *rénshēn (wren-shern)* 人参

girl	*nǚháizi (nwee-high-dzu)* 女孩子
girlfriend	*nǚpéngyou (nwee-perng-you)* 女朋友
glasses (eye)	*yǎnjìng (yahn-jeeng)* 眼镜
gloves	*shǒutào (show-tou)* 手套
gold	*jīn (jeen)* 金
goldfish	*jīnyú (jeen yuu)* 金鱼
golf	*gāoěrfūqiú (gow-urr-foo-cheo)* 高尔夫球
goose	*é (er)* 鹅
government office	*jīguān (jee gwahn)* 机关
gram	*kè (ker)* 克
grandfather	*zǔfù (zoo-foo)* 祖父
grandmother	*zǔmǔ (zoo-moo)* 祖母
grandparents	*zǔ fùmǔ (zoo-foo-moo)* 祖父母
grapes	*pútao (poo-taow)* 葡萄
grass	*cǎo (tsaow)* 草
great, big	*dà (dah)* 大
guest	*kèrén (ker-wren)* 客人
guest house	*bīnguǎn (been gwahn)* 宾馆
guide	*dǎoyóu (dow-you)* 导游
guidebook	*lǚyóu zhǐnán (lwee-you jr-nahn)* 旅游指南
gym	*tǐyùguǎn (tee-yuu-gwahn)* 体育馆
gymnastics	*tǐcāo (tee-tsow)* 体操
gynecologist	*fùkē yīshēng (foo-ker-ee-sherng)* 妇科医生

[H]

half	*bàn (bahn)* 半
hall (meeting)	*guǎn (gwahn)* 馆
handbag	*shǒutíbāo (show-tee-bow)* 手提包
handball	*shǒuqiú (show-cheo)* 手球
handicapped person	*cánjí rénshì (tsahn-jee wren shr)* 残疾人士
handicraft	*shǒugōngyìpǐn (show-gohng-ee-peen)* 手工艺品
hangover	*sù zuì (soo zway)* 宿醉
Happy Birthday	*Shēngrì kuàilè (sherng rr kwai ler)* 生日快乐
harvest	*shōuhuò (show-hoe)* 收获
hay fever	*kūcǎo rè (koo tsow ruh)* 枯草热
health club	*jiànshēn fáng (jee-an-shern fahng)* 健身房
heart attack	*xīnzàngbìng fāzuò (sheen-zahng-beeng fah-zwoh)* 心脏病发作
high school	*zhōngxué (johng shway)* 中学
highway	*gōnglù (gohng-loo)* 公路
hill	*xiǎo shān (shou-shahn)* 小山
history	*lìshǐ (lee-shr)* 历史
holiday	*jiàqī (jah-chee)* 假期
home	*jiā (jah)* 家
hometown	*gùxiāng (goo-she-ahng)* 故乡 / *jiāxiāng (jah-she-ahng)* 家乡
homosexual	*tóngxìngliàn (tohng-sheeng-lee-an)* 同性恋
honey	*fēngmì (ferng-mee)* 蜂蜜

Hong Kong	*Xiānggǎng (Shee-ahng Gahng)* 香港
horror (movie)	*kǒngbù piàn (kohng boo pee-an)* 恐怖片
house	*fángwū (fahng-woo)* 房屋
housewife	*jiātíng zhǔfù (jahteeng zoofoo)* 家庭主妇
HST (High-Speed Train)	*gāotiě (gow-tee-eh)* 高铁
hurry	*hěn jí (hern-jee)* 很急
husband	*zhàngfu (jahng-foo)* 丈夫
[I]	
ice	*bīng (beeng)* 冰
ice cream	*bīngqílín (beeng chee-leen)* 冰淇淋
ice skating	*huábīng (hwah beeng)* 滑冰
ice water	*bīng shuǐ (been shway)* 冰水
iced coffee	*bīng kāfēi (beeng kah-fay)* 冰咖啡
ID	*yònghù míng (yohng-hoo-meeng)* 用户名
illegal	*bù héfǎ (boo-her-fah)* 不合法
IMAX	*jù mù diànyǐng (jwee moo IMAX dee-an eeng)* 巨幕IMAX电影
important	*zhòngyào (johng-yee-ow)* 重要
impossible	*bù kěnéng (boo-ker-nerng)* 不可能
industry	*gōngyè (gohng-yeh)* 工业
inexpensive	*piányi (pee-an-ee)* 便宜
informal	*fēizhèngshì (fay-jern-shr)* 非正式
information (news)	*xiāoxi (she-ow-she)* 消息
information desk	*wènxùn chù (wern-shwun-choo)* 问讯处

injection	**zhùshè** (joo-sher) 注射
insurance	**bǎoxiǎn** (bow-shee-an) 保险
interesting	**yǒu yìsi** (you-ee-suh) 有意思
intermission	**mùjiān xiūxi** (moo-jee-an she-oh-she) 幕间休息
international	**guójì** (gwoh-jee) 国际
interpreter	**fānyì** (fahn-ee) 翻译
intersection (streets)	**shízì lùkǒu** (shr-dzu-loo-koe) 十字路口
invitation	**qǐngtiě** (cheeng-tee-eh) 请帖 / **qǐngjiǎn** (cheeng-jee-an) 请柬
invite	**yāoqǐng** (yee-ow-cheeng) 邀请
ivory	**xiàngyá** (shee-ahng-yah) 象牙

[J]

jacket	**duǎn shàngyī** (dwahn-shahng-ee) 短上衣
jade	**yù** (yuu) 玉
jail, prison	**jiānyù** (jee-an-yuu) 监狱
jazz	**juéshì** (jway-shr) 爵士
jeans	**niúzǎi kù** (new-zigh-koo) 牛仔裤
jewelry	**zhūbǎo** (joo-bow) 珠宝
jogging	**mànpǎo** (mahn-pow) 慢跑
joke (noun)	**xiàohuà** (shee-ow-hwah) 笑话
journalist	**jìzhě** (jee-juh) 记者
journey	**lǚxíng** (lwee-sheeng) 旅行
juice (fruit)	**guǒzhī** (gwoh-jr) 果汁
jumper/sweater	**máoyī** (mao-ee) 毛衣
jungle	**cónglín** (tsohng-leen) 丛林
justice	**gōngzhèng** (gohng-jerng) 公正

[K]

karaoke	*kǎlā OK (kah-lah-OK)* 卡拉OK
kelp / seaweed	*hǎidài (hi-die)* 海带
key	*yàoshi (yow-shr)* 钥匙
kilogram	*gōngjīn (gohng-jeen)* 公斤
kilometer	*gōnglǐ (gohng-lee)* 公里
kimchi	*Hánguó pàocài (pow-tsigh)* 韩国泡菜
kindergarten	*yòuéryuán (you-urr-ywahn)* 幼儿园
kiss	*wěn (wern)* 吻
kitchen	*chúfáng (choo-fahng)* 厨房
kite	*fēngzhēng (ferng-jerng)* 风筝
kleenex	*zhǐjīn (jr-jeen)* 纸巾
Korea (North)	*Cháoxiǎn (Chow-she-an)* 朝鲜
Korea (South)	*Hánguó (hahng-gwoh)* 韩国
Kyoto	*Jīngdū (Jeeng-doo)* 京都

[L]

lacquerware	*qīqì (chee-chee)* 漆器
lake	*hú (hoo)* 湖
lamb (meat)	*yángròu (yahng-row)* 羊肉
landlord	*fángzhǔ (fahng-joo)* 房主
language	*yǔyán (yuu-yahn)* 语言
late	*wǎn (wahn)* 晚
laundry bag	*xǐyī dài (she-ee die)* 洗衣袋
laundry form	*xǐyī dān (she-ee dahn)* 洗衣单
law	*fǎlǜ (fah-lwee)* 法律
lawyer	*lǜshī (lwee-shr)* 律师
leader	*lǐngdǎo (leeng-dow)* 领导
leave (depart)	*líkāi (lee-kigh)* 离开

leave a message	*liú huà (leo hwah)* 留话	
lecture	*jiǎngyǎn (jee-ahng-yahn)* 讲演	
leisure time	*kòngxián shíjiān (kohng-shee-an shr-jee-an)* 空闲时间	
letter	*xìn (sheen)* 信	
library	*túshūguǎn (too-shoo-gwahn)* 图书馆	
license	*zhùcè zhèng (joo-tser-zherng)* 注册证	
light rail transit/ LRT	*qīngguǐ (cheeng-gway)* 轻轨	
liquor	*báijiǔ (by-jeo)* 白酒	
literature	*wénxué (wern-shway)* 文学	
local dish	*dìfāng cài (dee-fahng tsigh)* 地方菜	
lock	*suǒ (swoh)* 锁	
longevity	*chángshòu (chahng-show)* 长寿	
Los Angeles	*Luòshānjī (Lwoh Shahn-jee)* 洛杉矶	
lost-and-found	*shīwù zhāolǐng (shr-woo jow-leeng)* 失物招领	
love (verb)	*ài (aye)* 爱	
LRT station	*qīngguǐ zhàn (cheeng-gway jahn)* 轻轨站	
luck	*yùnqi (ywun-chee)* 运气	
luggage	*xíngli (sheeng-lee)* 行李	
lunar calendar	*yīn lì (een lee)* 阴历	

[M]

Macao	*Àomén (Ow-mern)* 澳门
magazine	*zázhì (zah-jr)* 杂志
magic	*móshù (mwo-shoo)* 魔术

Maglev (magnetic levitation)   *cí xuánfú (tsu shwen-foo)* 磁悬浮

mahjong   *májiàng (mah-jee-ahng)* 麻将

mainland   *dàlù (dah-loo)* 大陆

main station   *zǒngzhàn (zohng jahn)* 总站

make up room (guest's request)   *qǐng dǎsǎo (cheeng dah-sao)* 请打扫

male   *nán (nahn)* 男

man, male   *nánrén (nahn-wren)* 男人

management   *guǎnlǐ (gwahn-lee)* 管理

manager   *jīnglǐ (jeeng-lee)* 经理

massage   *ànmó (ahn-mwo)* 按摩

mechanic   *jìgōng (jee-gohng)* 技工

message   *liú huà (leo-hwah)* 留话

microphone   *màikèfēng (my-ker-ferng)* 麦克风

Mid-Autumn Festival   *Zhōngqiūjié (Johng-chew jee-eh)* 中秋节

military   *jūnshì (jwin-shr)* 军事

milk   *niúnǎi (new-nigh)* 牛奶

mineral water   *kuàngquánshuǐ (kwahng-chwahn shway)* 矿泉水

mobile-Internet   *yídòng wǎng (ee-doong wahng)* 移动网

miniskirt   *chāoduǎnqún (chow dwahn-chwun)* 超短裙

model (fashion)   *mótèr (mwo-ter-urr)* 模特儿

monosodium glutamate   *wèijīng (way-jeeng)* 味精

Moscow   *Mòsīkē (Mwo-suh-ker)* 莫斯科

mountain	*shān (shahn)* 山
movie	*diànyǐng (dee-an eeng)* 电影
movie theater	*diànyǐngyuàn (dee-an-eeng ywahn)* 电影院
museum	*bówùguǎn (bwo-woo-gwahn)* 博物馆
music	*yīnyuè (een-yway)* 音乐
Muslim	*Huíjiàotú (Hway-jee-ow-too)* 回教徒

[N]

nap	*xiǎo shuì (shiaow-shway)* 小睡
nation	*guó (gwoh)* 国
national	*guójiā (gwoh-jah)* 国家
nationality	*guójí (gwoh-jee)* 国籍
native dress	*guófú (gwoh-foo)* 国服
neighbor	*línjū (leen-jwee)* 邻居
new	*xīn (sheen)* 新
news	*xīnwén (sheen-wern)* 新闻
newspaper	*bàozhǐ (bow-jr)* 报纸
New Year	*Xīnnián (Sheen Nee-an)* 新年
New Year's day	*Yuándàn (Ywahn-dahn)* 元旦
New Year's Eve	*Chúxī (Chwoo She)* 除夕
nightclub	*yèzǒnghuì (Yeh johng-hway)* 夜总会
noodles	*miàn (mee-an)* 面
north	*běi (bay)* 北
North America	*Běiměi zhōu (Bay May-joe)* 北美洲
nuclear	*hé (her)* 核
nurse	*hùshi (hoo-shr)* 护士
nursery	*tuōérsuǒ (twoh-urr-swoh)* 托儿所

[O]

oatmeal	*màipiàn (my-pee-an)*	麦片
occupation	*zhíyè (jr-yeh)*	职业
ocean	*hǎiyáng (high-yahng)*	海洋
office	*bàngōngshì (bahn-gohng-shr)*	办公室
official (bureaucrat)	*guān (gwahn)*	官
offline	*bú zàixiàn (boo zigh-shee-an)*	不在线
old (person)	*lǎo (lao)*	老
online	*zàixiàn (zigh-shee-an)*	在线
one-way	*dānchéng (dahn-cherng)*	单程
open	*kāimén (kigh-mern)*	开门
opera	*gējù (ger-jwee)*	歌剧
orange juice	*júzi zhī (jwee-dzu jr)*	桔子汁
outlet (electric)	*chāzuò (chah-zwoh)*	插座
overcoat	*dàyī (dah-ee)*	大衣
overseas	*guówài (gwoh-wigh)*	国外
Overseas Chinese	*Huáqiáo (Hwah Chee-ow)*	华侨
owner	*wùzhǔ (woo-zoo)*	物主

[P]

Pacific Ocean	*Tàipíngyáng (Tie-peeng Yahng)*	太平洋
package	*bāoguǒ (bow-gwoh)*	包裹
pagoda	*bǎotǎ (bow-tah)*	宝塔
palace	*gōngdiàn (gohng-dee-an)*	宫殿
panda	*xióngmāo (shee-ong mao)*	熊猫
Paris	*Bālí (Bah-lee)*	巴黎

parking lot	*tíngchē chǎng (teeng-cher chahng)* 停车场
party (recreational)	*jùhuì (jwee-hway)* 聚会
passenger	*lǚkè (lwee-ker)* 旅客
passport	*hùzhào (hoo-jow)* 护照
passport number	*hùzhào hàomǎ (hoo-jow how-mah)* 护照号码
password	*mìmǎ (me-mah)* 密码
pastry	*gāodiǎn (gow-dee-an)* 糕点
peace	*hépíng (her-peeng)* 和平
peanuts	*huāshēng (hwah-sherng)* 花生
Pearl River	*Zhūjiāng (Joo Jee-ahang)* 珠江
pearls	*zhēnzhū (zhern-joo)* 珍珠
Peking Duck	*Běijīng kǎoyā (Bay-jeeng kow-yah)* 北京烤鸭
penicillin	*qīngméisù (cheeng-may-soo)* 青霉素
performance	*yǎnchū (yahn-choo)* 演出
performer	*yǎnyuán (yahn-ywahn)* 演员
permission	*xǔkě (she-ker)* 许可
pharmacy	*yàodiàn (yow-dee-an)* 药店
physical exam	*tǐjiǎn (tee jee-an)* 体检
pingpong	*pīngpāngqiú (peeng-pahng-cheo)* 乒乓球
platform (train)	*zhàntái (jahn-tie)* 站台
play (theatrical)	*xìjù (she-jwee)* 戏剧
playground	*cāochǎng (tsow-chahng)* 操场
police station	*gōng'ānjú (gohng-ahn jwee)* 公安局
pollution	*wūrǎn (woo-rahn)* 污染

popular music	*liúxíng yīnyue (lü-sheen een-yway)* 流行音乐
population	*rénkǒu (wren-koe)* 人口
porridge	*zhōu (joe)* 粥
pottery	*táoqì (tou-chee)* 陶器
premier (country)	*zǒnglǐ (zohng-lee)* 总理
prescription	*yàofāng (yee-ow-fahng)* 药方
president (company)	*zǒngcái (zohng-tsigh)* 总裁
president (country)	*zǒngtǒng (zohng-tohng)* 总统
printed matter	*yìnshuā pǐn (een-shwah peen)* 印刷品
prison	*jiānyù (jee-an-yuu)* 监狱
profession	*zhíyè (jr-yeh)* 职业
prostitute	*jìnǚ (jee-nwee)* 妓女
province	*shěng (sherng)* 省
public	*gōnggòng (gohng-gohng)* 公共
public square	*guǎngchǎng (gwahng chahng)* 广场
pudding	*bùdīng (boo-deeng)* 布丁
purse, handbag	*shǒutíbāo (show-tee-bow)* 手提包
[Q]	
quality	*zhìliàng (jr-lee-ahng)* 质量
quantity	*shùliàng (shoo-lee-ahng)* 数量
question	*wèntí (wern-tee)* 问题
queue	*páiduì (pie-dway)* 排队
quick, fast	*kuài (kwie)* 快
quiet, peaceful	*ānjìng (ahn-jeeng)* 安静

[R]

race (human)	*zhǒngzú (johng-joo)* 种族
racism	*zhǒngzú piānjiàn (johng-joo-pee-an-jee-an)* 种族偏见
raincoat	*yǔyī (yuu-ee)* 雨衣
rap music	*ráoshé (rao-sher)* 饶舌
rape	*qiángjiān (chee-ahng-jee-an)* 强奸
receipt	*shōujù (show-jwee)* 收据
reception, party	*zhāodài huì (jow-die-hway)* 招待会
recharge (battery)	*chōng diàn (chohng-dee-an)* 充电
refund	*tuīkuǎn (tway-kwahn)* 推款
region	*dìqū (dee-chwee)* 地区
relative, kin	*qīnqi (cheen-chee)* 亲戚
repair	*xiū (shew)* 修
resident permit	*jūliú zhèng (jwee-leo zherng)* 居留证
rest	*xiūxi (shew-she)* 休息
reverse charges	*duìfāng fùfèi (dway-fahng-foo-fay)* 对方付费
rice (cooked)	*báifàn (by-fahn)* 白饭
rich	*fùyǒu (foo-you)* 富有
ring (jewelry)	*jièzhi (jeh-jr)* 戒指
river	*hé (her)* 河
road	*lù (loo)* 路
roast suckling pig	*kǎo rǔ zhū (kow roo-joo)* 烤乳猪
Romance (movie)	*yánqíng piàn (yahn cheeng pee-an)* 言情片

room key	*yàoshi (yee-ow shr)* 钥匙	
room number	*fángjiān hàomǎ (fahng-jee-an how-mah)* 房间号码	
round-trip	*láihuí (lie-hway)* 来回	
round-trip ticket	*láihuí piào (lie-hway pee-ow)* 来回票	
row, line, queue	*pái (pie)* 排	
rugby	*gǎnlǎnqiú (gahn-lahn chew)* 橄榄球	
ruins	*fèixū (fay-shee)* 废墟	
[S]		
safe (adjective)	*ānquán (ahn-chwahn)* 安全	
safe (noun)	*bǎoxiǎn xiāng (bow-she-an-she-ahng)* 保险箱	
saké (liquor)	*Rìběn jiǔ (rr-burn jew)* 日本酒	
sales tax	*yíngyè shuì (eeng-yeh shway)* 营业税	
sandwich	*sānmíngzhì (sahn-meeng-jr)* 三明治	
San Francisco	*Jiùjīnshān (Jeo-jeen Shahn)* 旧金山	
sashimi	*cì shēn (tsu-shern)* 刺身	
satellite	*wèixīng (way-sheeng)* 卫星	
sausage	*xiāngcháng (shee-ahng chahng)* 香肠	
scallops	*gānbèi (gahn-bay)* 干贝	
scenery	*fēngjǐng (ferng-jeeng)* 风景	
school	*xuéxiào (shway-she-ow)* 学校	
Science fiction (movie)	*kēhuàn piàn (ker hwahn pee-an)* 科幻片	
scientist	*kēxuéjiā (ker-shway-jah)* 科学家	

seafood	*hǎixiān (high-she-an)* 海鲜	
secretary	*mìshū (me-shoo)* 秘书	
security guard	*ānquán rényuán (ahn-chwahn wren-ywahn)* 安全人员	
seminar	*yántǎo huì (yahn-tow-hway)* 研讨会	
Seoul	*Shǒuěr (Show-ur)* 首尔	
service fee	*fúwù fèi (foo-woo fay)* 服务费	
set meal	*tàocān (tao-tsahn)* 套餐	
sex (gender)	*xìng (sheeng)* 性	
ship	*chuán (chwahn)* 船	
shopping area	*shāngyè qū (shahng-yeh-chwee)* 商业区	
Siberia	*Xībólìyà (She-bwo-lee-yah)* 西伯利亚	
signature	*qiānmíng (chee-an meeng)* 签名	
singer	*gēshǒu (guh-shoo)* 歌手	
single room	*dānrén fáng (dahn-wren fahng)* 单人房	
Singles' day	*Guānggùnjié (Gwahng-goon jee-eh)* 光棍节	
Silk Road	*Sīchóu zhī lù (Suh-choe Jr Loo)* 丝绸之路	
sleep	*shuìjiào (shway-jee-ow)* 睡觉	
smartphone	*zhìnéng shǒujī (jr-nerng show-jee)* 智能手机	
soccer	*zúqiú (joo-chew)* 足球	
society	*shèhuì (sher-hway)* 社会	
soda water	*qìshuǐ (chee shway)* 汽水	
soft drink	*ruǎn xìng yǐnliào (rwahn-xeeng-ahng een-lee-ow)* 软性饮料	

soldier	*zhànshì (jahn-shr)* 战士	
south	*nán (nahn)* 南	
South China Sea	*Nánhǎi (Nahn High)* 南海	
souvenir	*jìniànpǐn (jee-nee-an-peen)* 纪念品	
souvenir shop	*jìniànpǐn diàn (jee-nee-an-peen dee-an)* 纪念品店	
space shuttle	*hángtiān fēijī (hahng-tee-an fay-jee)* 航天飞机	
specialty	*zhāopái cài (jow-pie tsigh)* 招牌菜	
spirits	*lièjiǔ (lee-ah jew)* 烈酒	
sports	*yùndòng (yuun-dohng)* 运动	
stadium	*tǐyù chǎng (tee-yuu-chahng)* 体育场	
stereo	*yīnxiǎng (een-shee-ahng)* 音响	
straw	*xīguǎn (she-gwahn)* 吸管	
study	*shūfáng (shoo-fahng)* 书房	
study abroad	*liúxué (lew-shway)* 留学	
subway card	*dìtiě kǎ (dee-tee-eh kah)* 地铁卡	
subway ticket	*dìtiě piào (dee-tee-eh pee-ow)* 地铁票	
suit (Western wear)	*xīfú (she-foo)* 西服	
suite	*tàofáng (tao fahng)* 套房	
sunglasses	*mòjìng (mo-jeeng)* 墨镜	
swimming	*yóuyǒng (you-yohng)* 游泳	
swimming pool	*yóuyǒngchí (you-yohng chr)* 游泳池	
symphony	*jiāoxiǎngyuè (jow-she-ahng-yway)* 交响乐	

[T]

table tennis   *pīngpāngqiú (peeng-pahng-cheo)* 乒乓球

taste, flavor   *wèi (way)* 味

tax free   *miǎn shuì (mee-an shway)* 免税

teacher   *jiàoshī (jow-shr)* 教师

teahouse   *cháguǎn (chah-gwahn)* 茶馆

technology transfer   *jìshù zhuǎnràng (jee-shoo jwahn-rahng)* 技术转让

television   *diànshì (dee-an-shr)* 电视

temple   *sìyuàn (suh-ywahn)* 寺院

tennis   *wǎngqiú (wahng-chew)* 网球

text (phone)   *duǎnxìn (dwahn-sheen)* 短信

Thailand   *Tàiguó (Tie-gwoh)* 泰国

theater   *jùchǎng (jwee-chahng)* 剧场

theater tickets   *xì piào (she-pee-ow)* 戏票

Tibet   *Xīzàng (She-zahng)* 西藏

tiger   *lǎohǔ (lao-hoo)* 老虎

tip (gratuity)   *xiǎofèi (shiaow-fay)* 小费

today's special   *jīnrì tècān (jeen-rr ter-tsahn)* 今日特餐

toilet paper   *cè zhǐ (tzer jr)* 厕纸

Tokyo   *Dōngjīng (Dohng-jeeng)* 东京

tour   *lǚxíng (lwee-sheeng)* 旅行

tour escort   *lǐngduì (leeng-dway)* 领队

tour group   *lǚxíng tuán (lwee-sheeng-twahn)* 旅行团

tourist   *lǚkè (lwee-kuh)* 旅客

tournament   *bǐsài (bee-sigh)* 比赛

trade fair	*jiāoyì huì (jow-ee hway)*	交易会
trademark	*shāngbiāo (shahg bee-ow)*	商标
translate, translator	*fānyì (yuán) (fahn-ee (ywahn))* 翻译(员)	
transportation	*yùnshū (ywun-shoo)*	运输
transportation charges	*yùnshū fèiyòng (ywun-shoo fay-yohng)* 运输费用	
tutor	*dǎoshī (dow-shr)*	导师
twin room	*shuāngchuáng fáng (shwahng chwang fahng)* 双床房	
Twitter	*tuītè (Twitter/tway-ter)*	推特
typhoon	*táifēng (tie-ferng)*	台风
[U]		
umbrella	*yǔsǎn (yuu-sahn)*	雨伞
unacceptable	*bùxíng (boo-sheeng)*	不行
uncle	*bófù (bwo-foo)*	伯父
uncomfortable	*bù shūfu (boo-shoo-foo)*	不舒服
uniform	*zhìfú (jr-foo)*	制服
United Nations	*Liánhéguó (Lee-an-her Gwoh)* 联合国	
United States	*Měiguó (May-gwoh)*	美国
universe	*yǔzhòu (yuu-joe)*	宇宙
urinate	*xiǎobiàn (shiaow-bee-an)*	小便
[V]		
vacancy	*kòng fáng (kohng-fahng)*	空房
Valentine's Day	*Qíngrénjié (Cheeng-wren jee-eh)* 情人节	
vacation	*fàngjià (fahng-jah)*	放假
vegetarian	*sùshí (soo-shr)*	素食

venereal disease	*xìngbìng (sheeng-beeng)*	性病
video-chat	*shìpín liáotiān (shr-peen lee-ow-tee-an)*	视频聊天
Vietnam	*Yuènán (Yway-nahn)*	越南
villa	*biéshù (bee-eh-shoo)*	别墅
village	*cūnzhuāng (tswun-jwahng)*	村庄
voice-chat	*yǔyīn liáotiān (yuu-een lee-ow-tee-an)*	语音聊天
volleyball	*páiqiú (pie-cheo)*	排球
vomit	*ǒutù (oh-too)*	呕吐
[W]		
wage, salary	*gōngzī (gohng-dzu)*	工资
waiting room	*hòuchē shì (hoe-cher shr)*	候车室
wallet	*píjiāzi (pee-jah-dzu)*	皮夹子
wall poster	*qiángbào (cheen-ahng bow)*	墙报
war	*zhànzhēng (jahn-jerng)*	战争
water	*shuǐ (shway)*	水
watermelon	*xīguā (she-gwah)*	西瓜
wealthy	*yǒu qián (yoe-chee-an)*	有钱
Wechat	*Wēixìn (Way-sheen)*	微信
wedding	*hūnlǐ (hwun-lee)*	婚礼
weekend	*zhōumò (joe-mwo)*	周末
Weibo	*Wēibó (Way-bwo)*	微博
welcome	*huānyíng (hwahn-eeng)*	欢迎
west	*xī (she)*	西
West (world)	*Xībiān (She-bee-an)*	西边
Western (movie)	*Xībù piàn (She boo pee-an)*	西部片

Western country	*Xīyáng (She-yahng)* 西洋
Western toilet	*zuòshì cèsuǒ (Tswoh-shr tser-swoh)* 坐式厕所
wildlife	*yěshēng dòngwù (yeh-sherng-dohng-woo)* 野生动物
wind	*fēng (ferng)* 风
windy	*guāfēng (gwah-ferng)* 刮风
wine	*pútaojiǔ (poo tou jew)* 葡萄酒
world	*shìjiè (shr-jeh)* 世界
wristwatch	*shǒubiǎo (show bee-ow)* 手表
writer	*zuòjiā (zwoh-jah)* 作家
[X]	
xerox	*fùyìn (foo-een)* 复印
x-ray	*X-guāng piànzi (x-gwahng-pee-an-dzu)* x-光片子
[Y]	
Yangtze River	*Chángjiāng (Chahng Jee-ahng)* 长江
Yellow River	*Huánghé (Hwahng Her)* 黄河
yogurt	*suānnǎi (swahn-nahn)* 酸奶
young	*niánqīng (nee-an-cheeng)* 年轻
youth	*qīngnián (chee-ahng-nee-an)* 青年
[Z]	
zero	*líng (leeng)* 零
zipper	*lāliàn (lah-lee-an)* 拉链
zoo	*dòngwùyuán (dohng-woo-ywahn)* 动物园

The Tuttle Story:
"Books to Span the East and West"

Many people are surprised to learn that the world's leading publisher of books on Asia had humble beginnings in the tiny American state of Vermont. The company's founder, Charles Tuttle, belonged to a New England family steeped in publishing.

Immediately after WWII, Tuttle served in Tokyo under General Douglas MacArthur and was tasked with reviving the Japanese publishing industry. He later founded the Charles E. Tuttle Publishing Company, which thrives today as one of the world's leading independent publishers.

Though a westerner, Tuttle was hugely instrumental in bringing a knowledge of Japan Asia to a world hungry for information about the East. By the time of his death in 1993, Tut had published over 6,000 books on Asian culture, history and art—a legacy honored by the Japanese emperor with the "Order of the Sacred Treasure," the highest tribute Japan can bestow upon a non-Japanese.

With a backlist of 1,500 titles, Tuttle Publishing is more active today than at any time in its past—still inspired by Charles Tuttle's core mission to publish fine books to span the E and West and provide a greater understanding of each.

Published by Tuttle Publishing, an imprint of Periplus Editions (HK) Ltd.

www.tuttlepublishing.com

Copyright © 2004, 2015 Boyé Lafayette De Mente

LCC Card No. 2003110054
ISBN 978-0-8048-4537-3

Distributed by:

North America, Latin America & Europe
Tuttle Publishing
364 Innovation Drive, North Clarendon,
VT 05759-9436, USA
Tel: 1 (802) 773 8930; Fax: 1 (802) 773 6993
info@tuttlepublishing.com
www.tuttlepublishing.com

Japan
Tuttle Publishing
Yaekari Building 3rd Floor, 5-4-12 Osaki,
Shinagawa-ku, Tokyo 1410032, Japan
Tel: (81) 3 5437 0171; Fax: (81) 3 5437 07
sales@tuttle.co.jp; www.tuttle.co.jp

Asia Pacific
Berkeley Books Pte Ltd
61 Tai Seng Avenue #02-12,
Singapore 534167
Tel: (65) 6280 1330; Fax: (65) 6280 6290
inquiries@periplus.com.sg; www.periplus.c

Indonesia
PT Java Books Indonesia
Jl. Rawa Gelam IV No. 9
Kawasan Industri Pulogadung
Jakarta 13930, Indonesia
Tel: 62 (21) 4682 1088; Fax: 62 (21) 461 0
crm@periplus.co.id; www.periplus.com

18 17 16 15   5 4 3 2 1   150
Printed in Singapore

TUTTLE PUBLISHING® is a registered trademark of Tuttle Publishing, a division of Periplus Editions (HK) Ltd.

31901056960984